This book belong to:
_____

ABOUT THIS BOOK

Thank you for purchasing this quality coloring book from Nicholas Nicky!

Inside this book are 50 unique and fun Dream Catcher coloring pages designed especially for kids.

Each image is on its own page with a BLANK backside to help avoid color bleed-through if you color with markers or other ink based pens.

If you use something other than colored pencils or crayons, we also recom-mend placing a sheet of paper or some other blotter between your coloring page and the one beneath it while you work.

We hope you enjoy your
Dream Catcher Coloring Book!

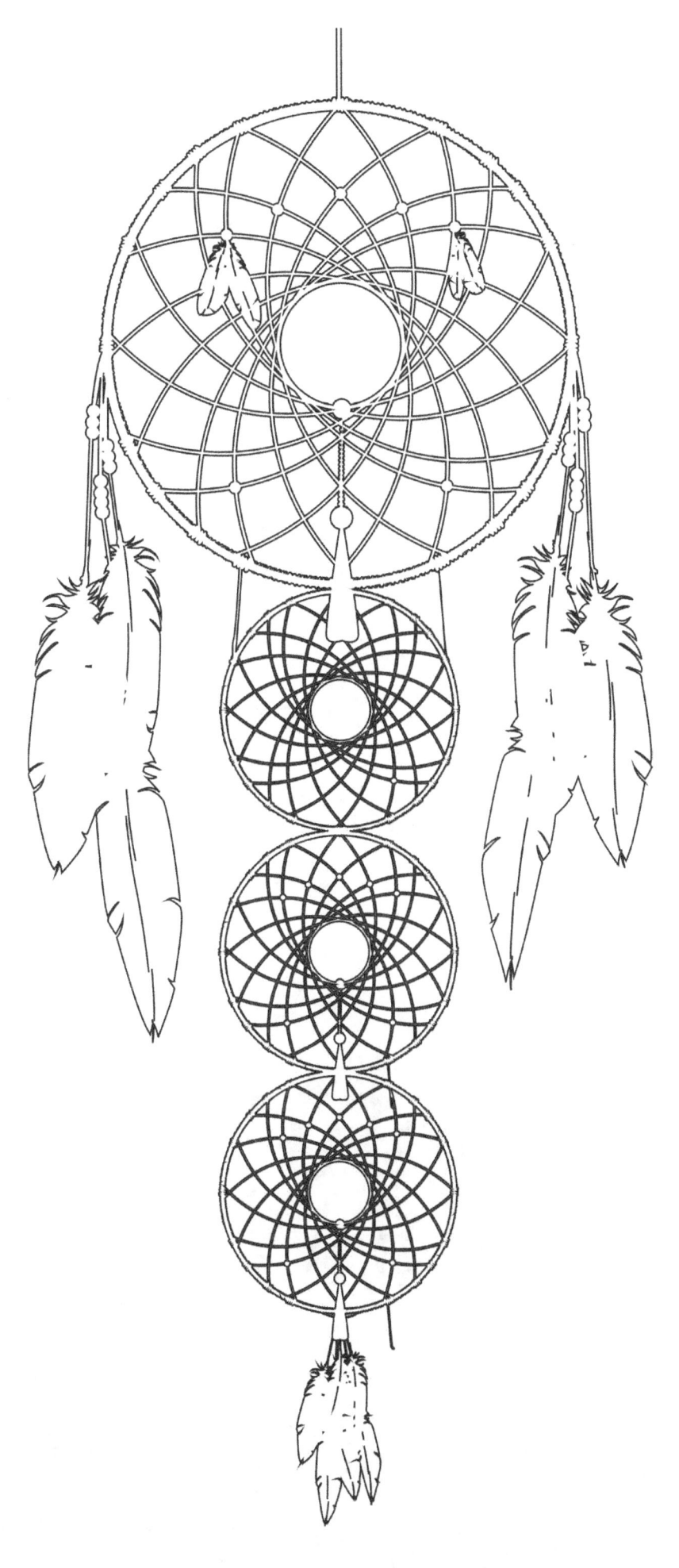

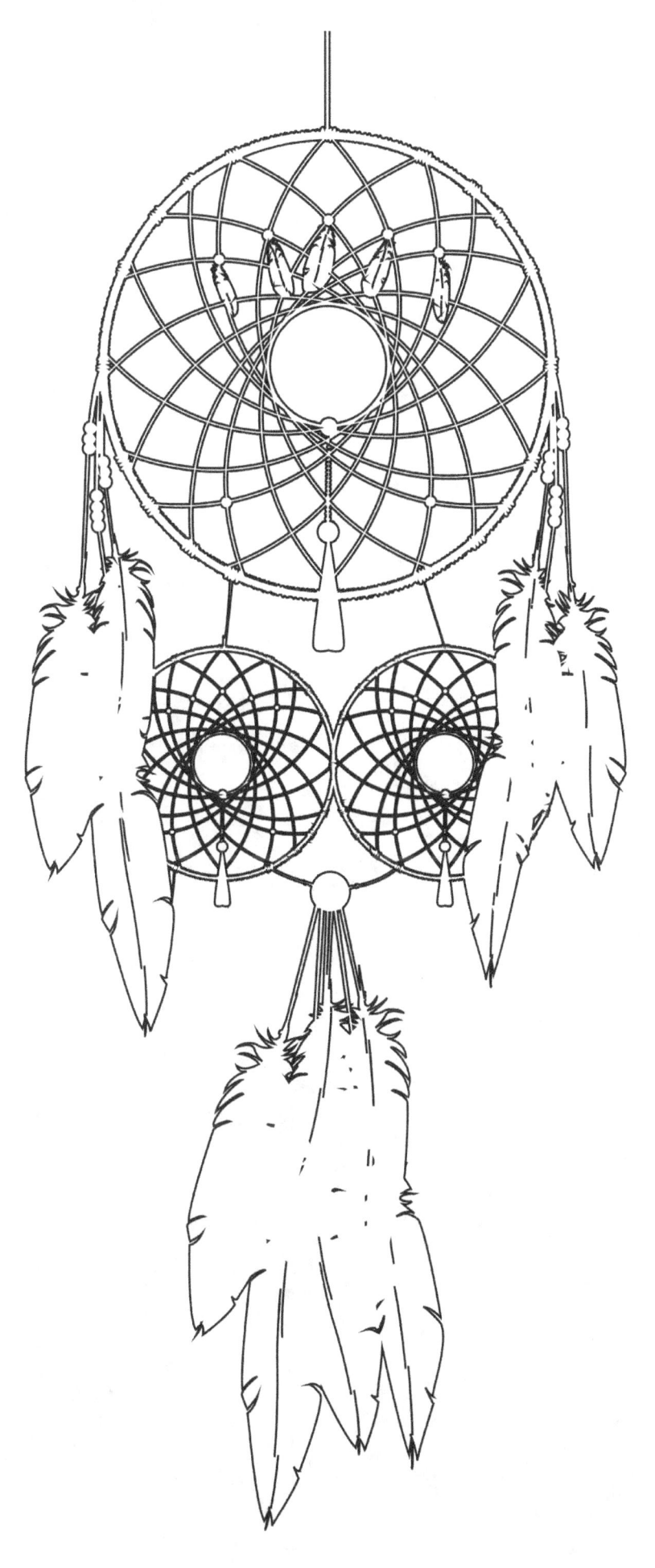

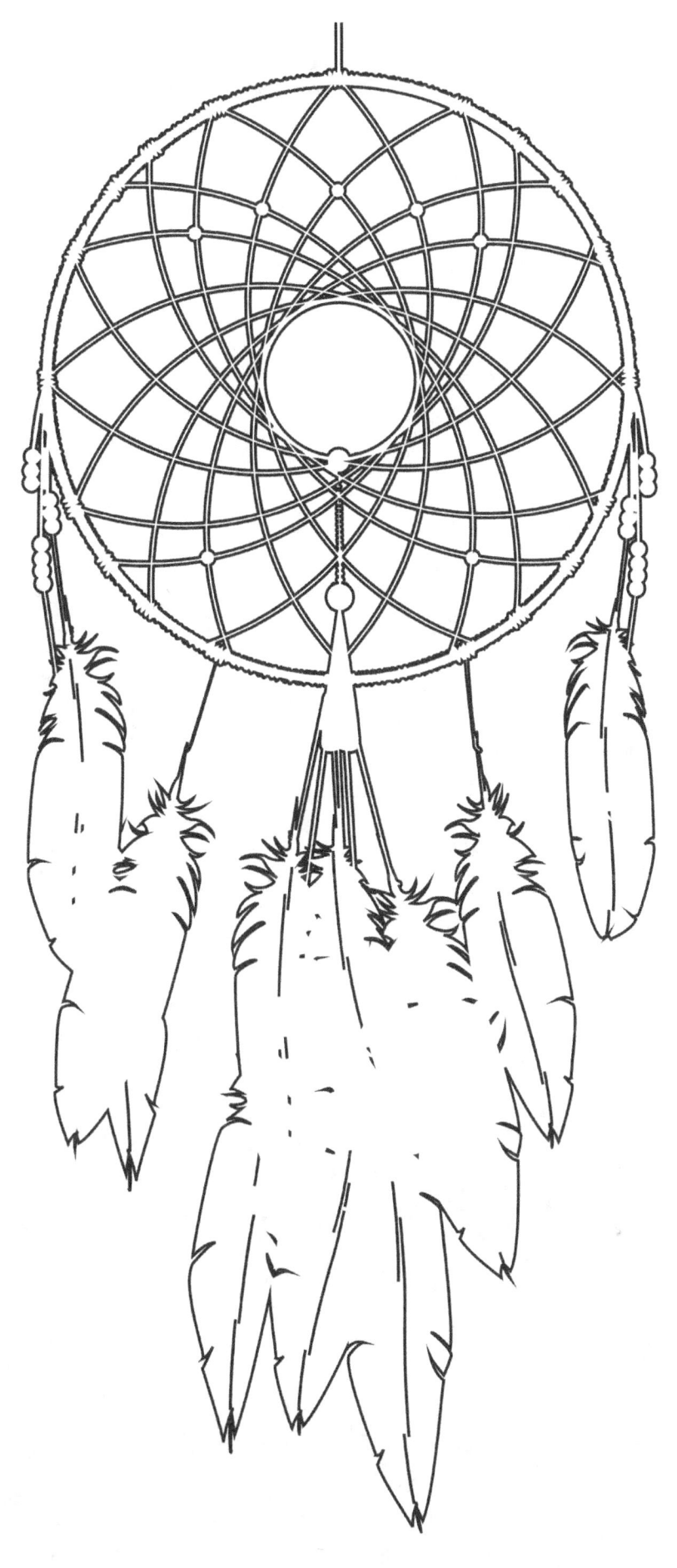

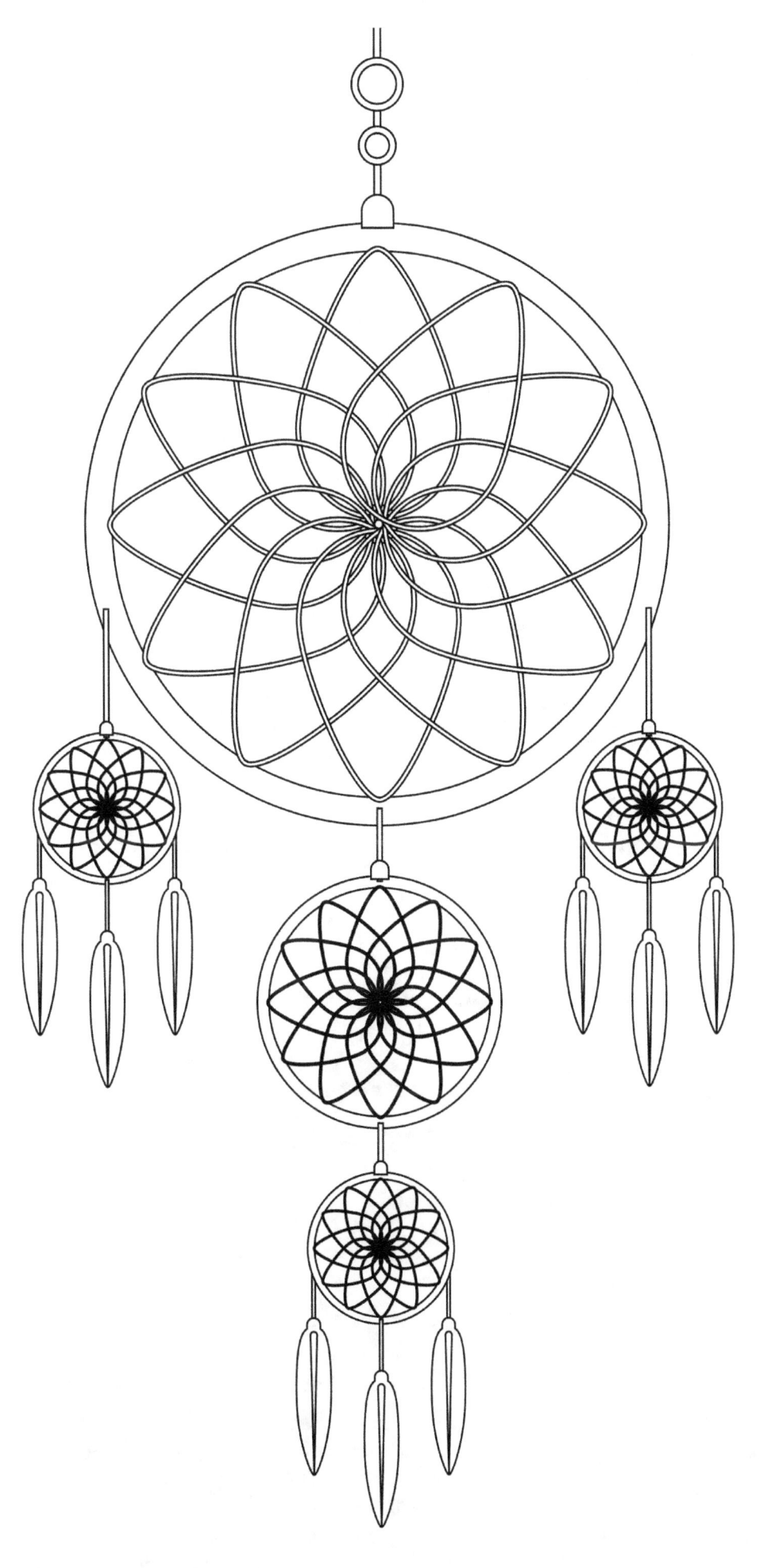

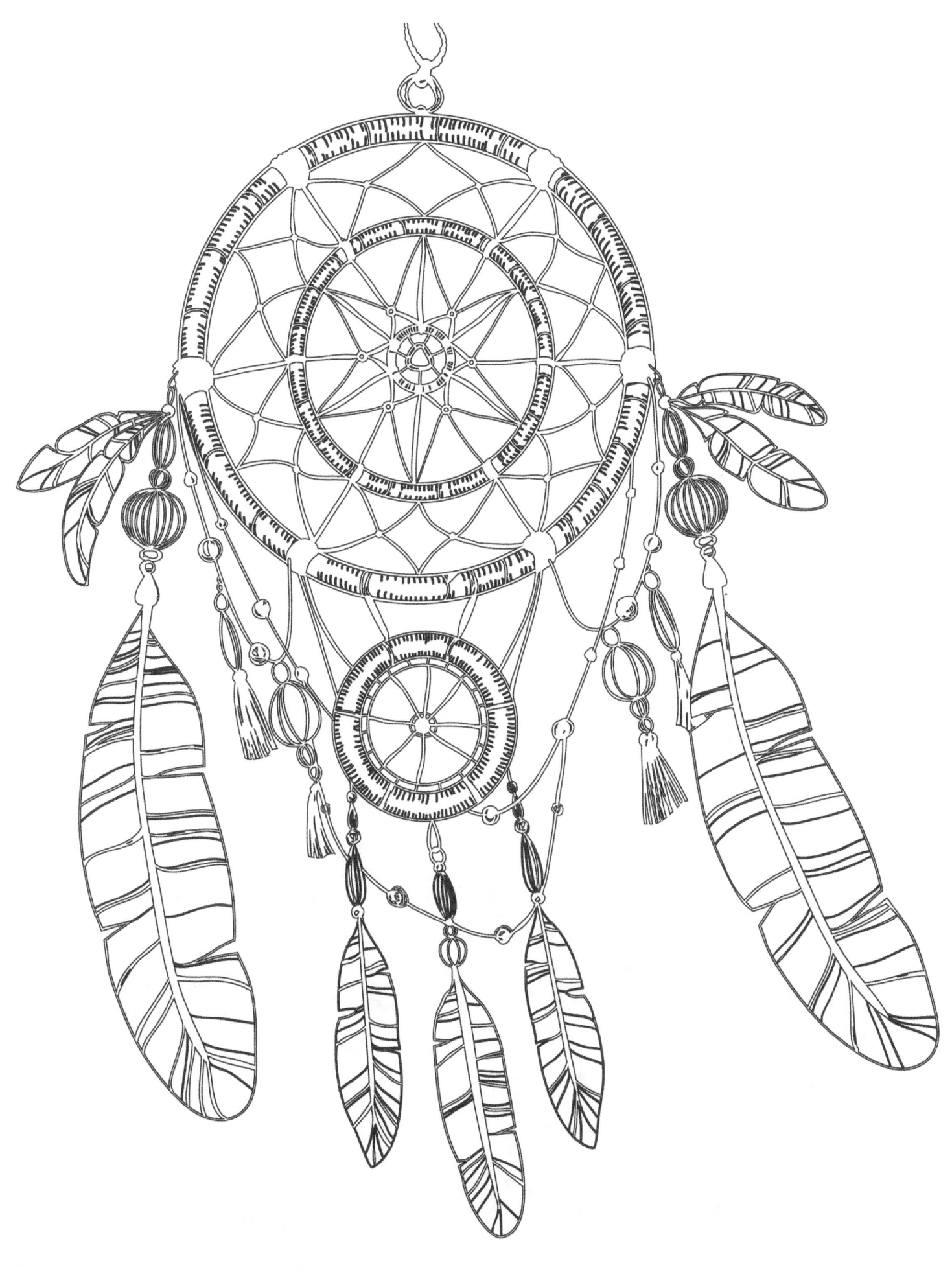

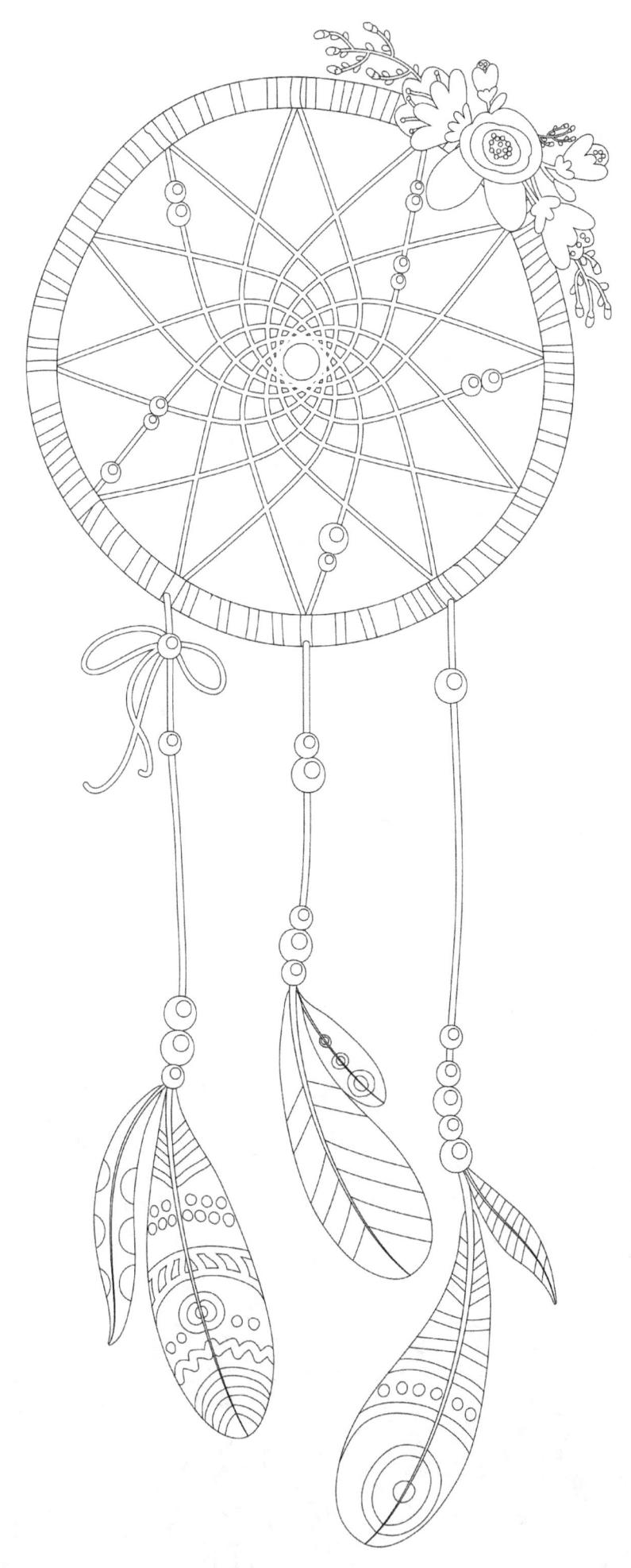

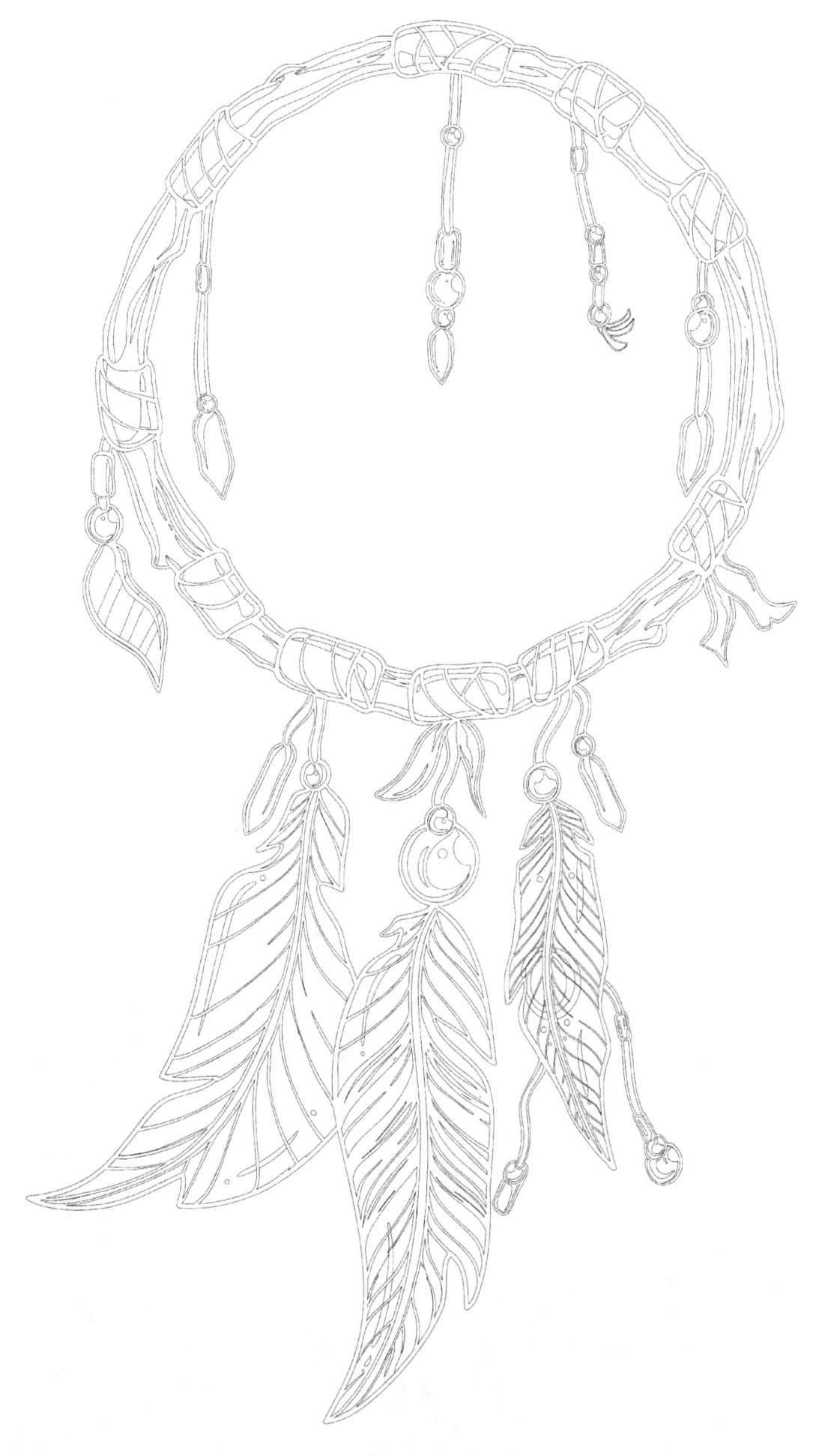

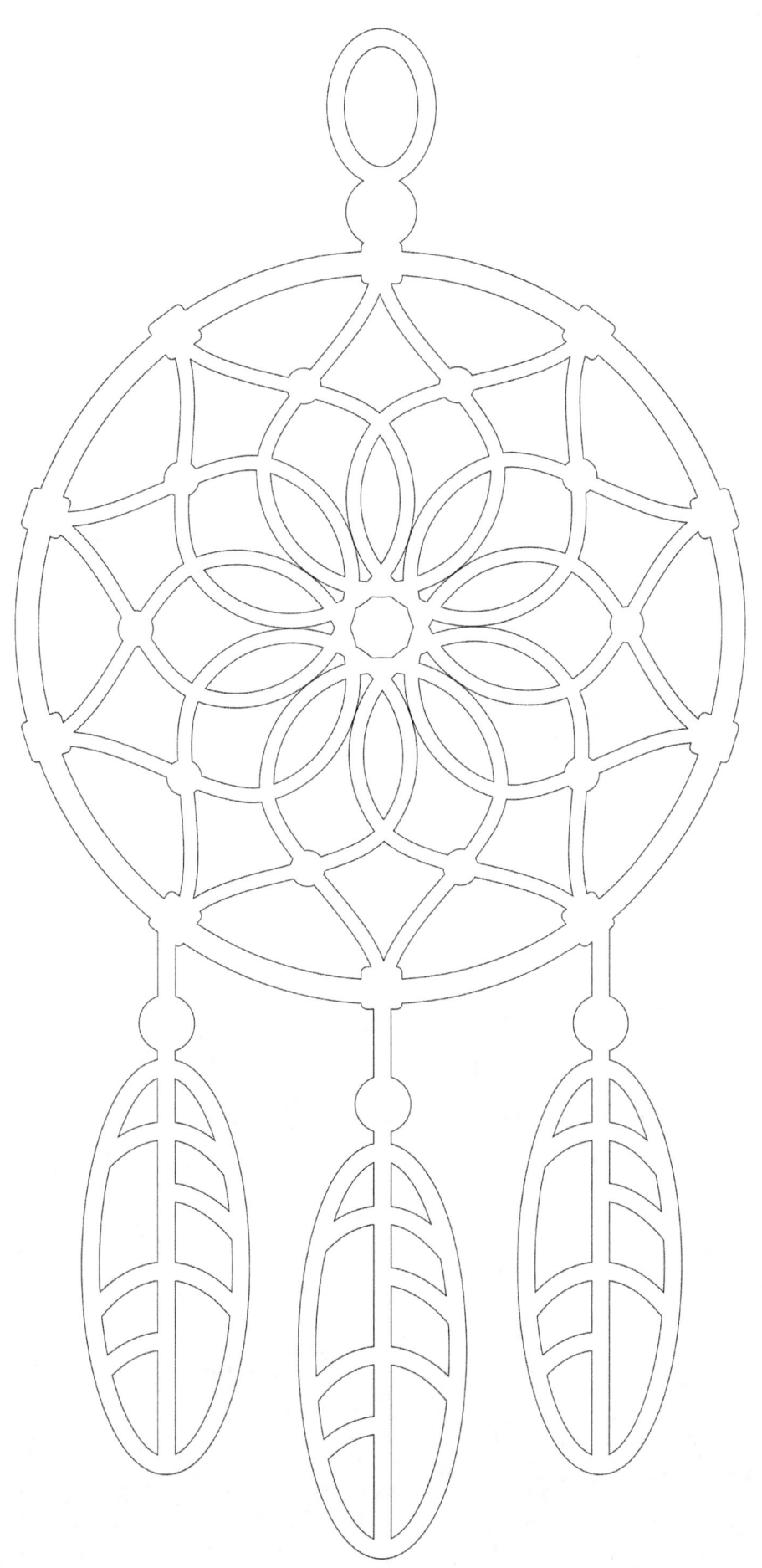

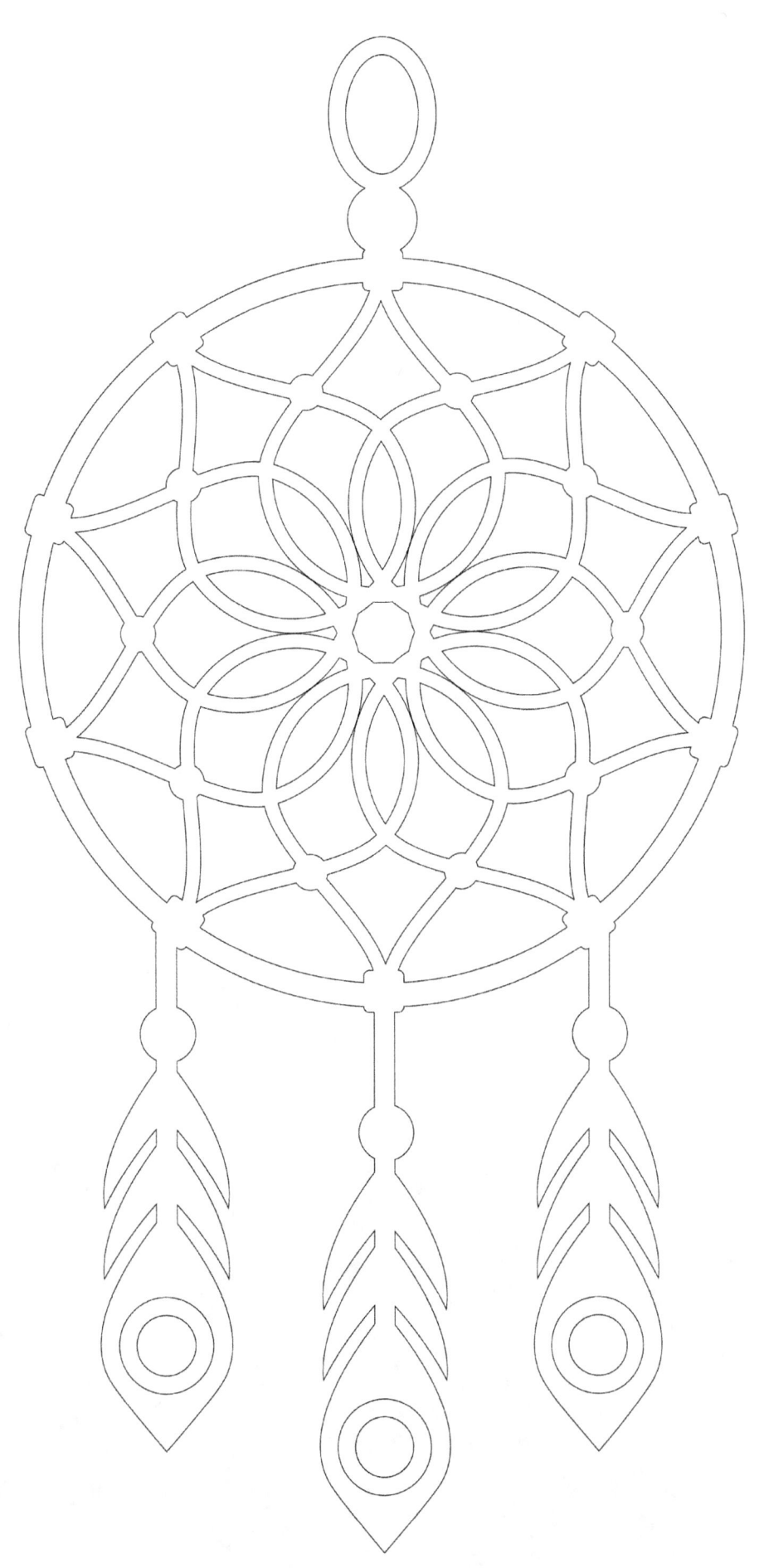

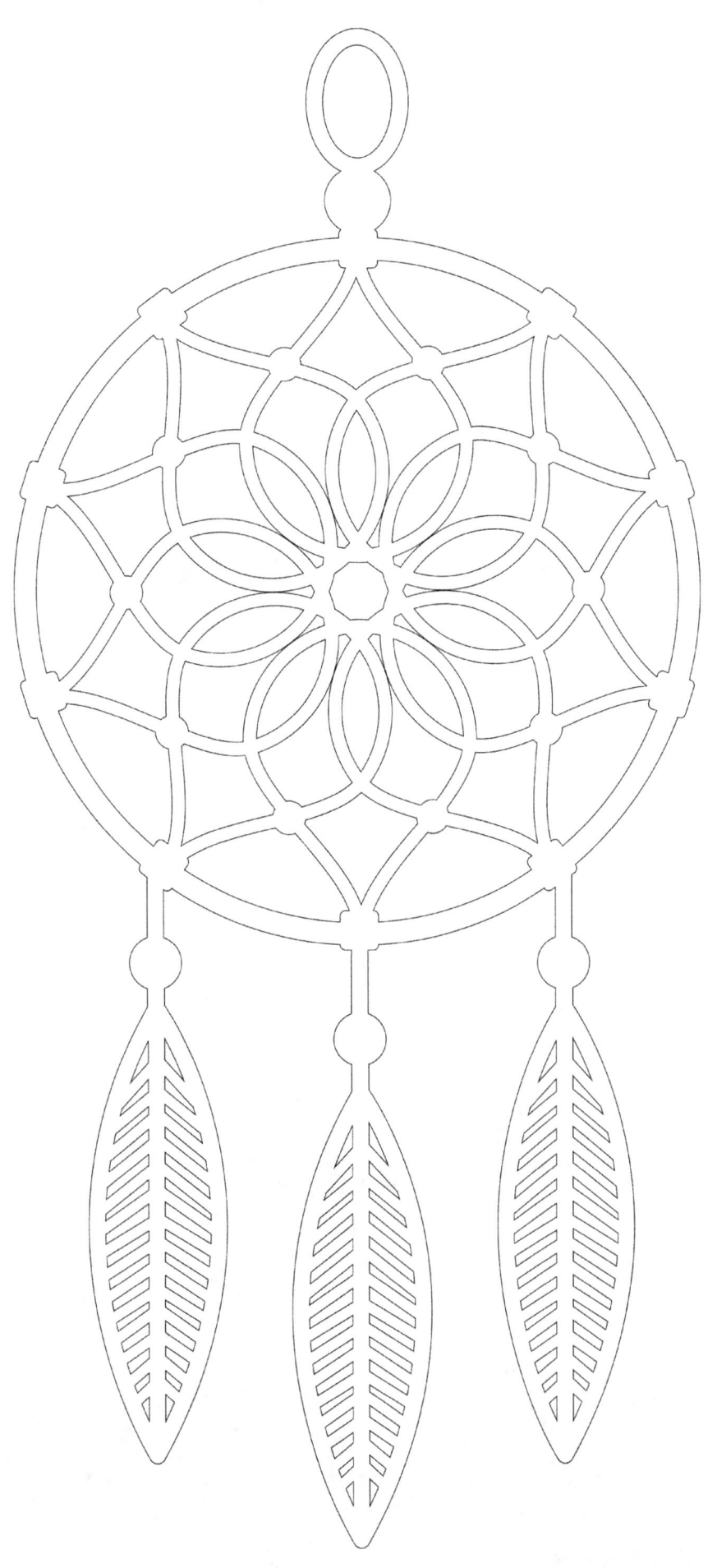

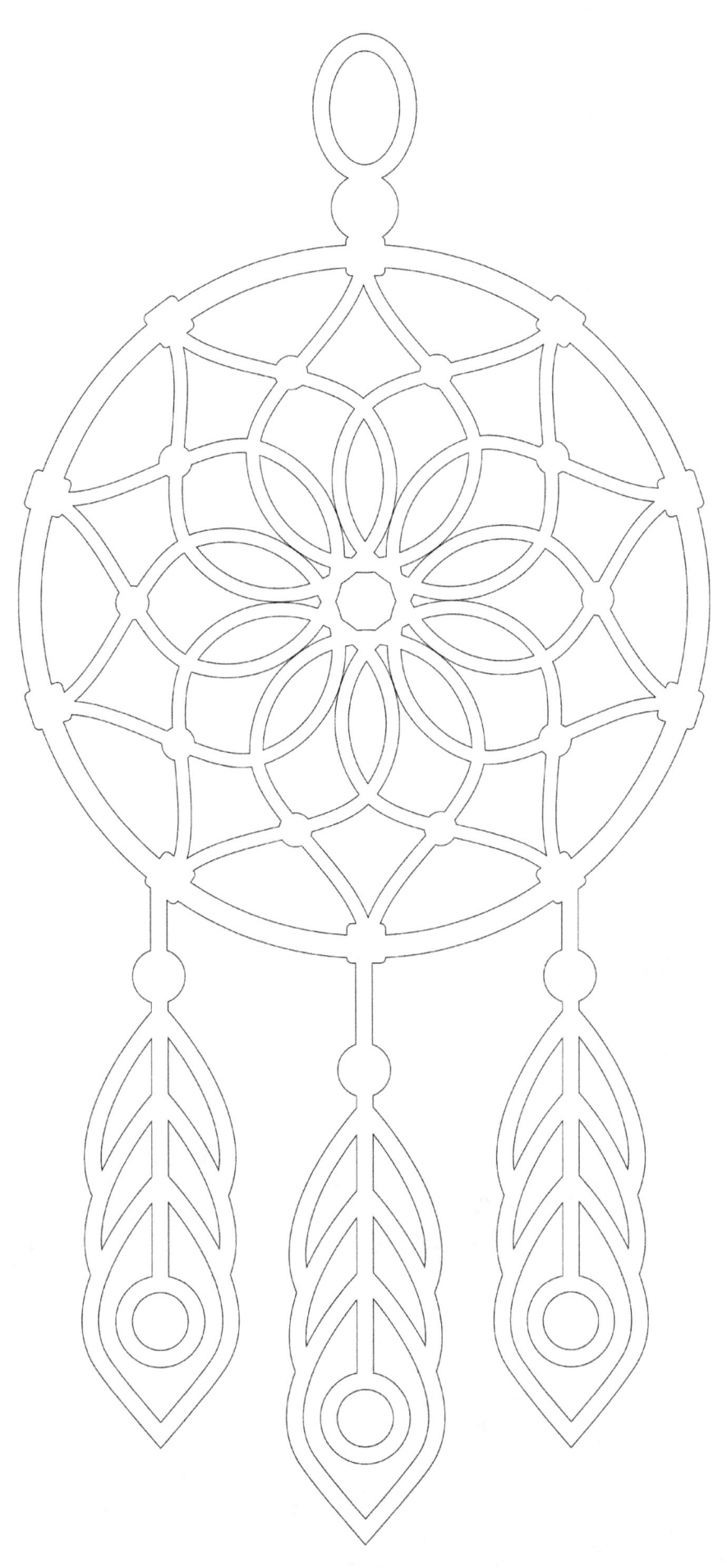

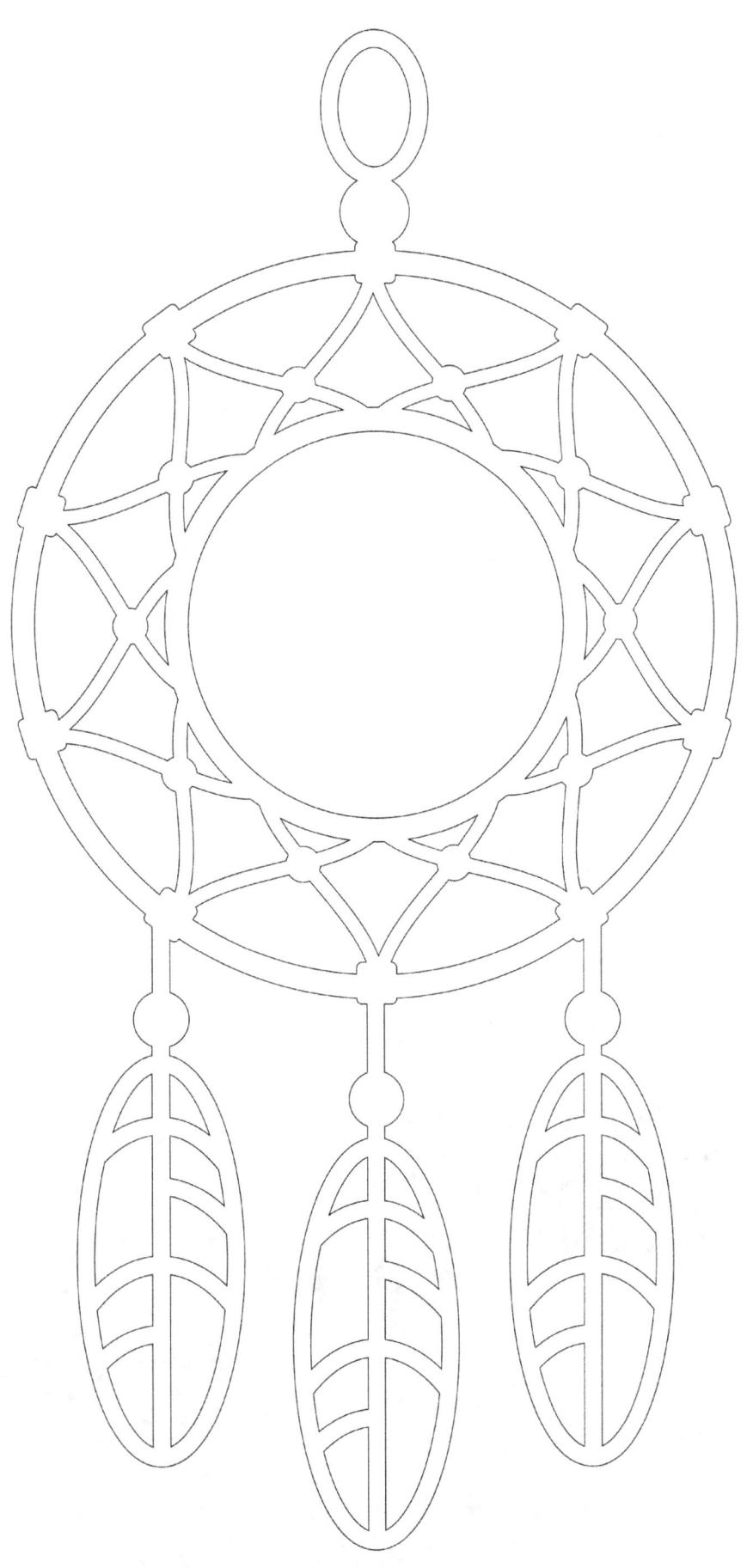

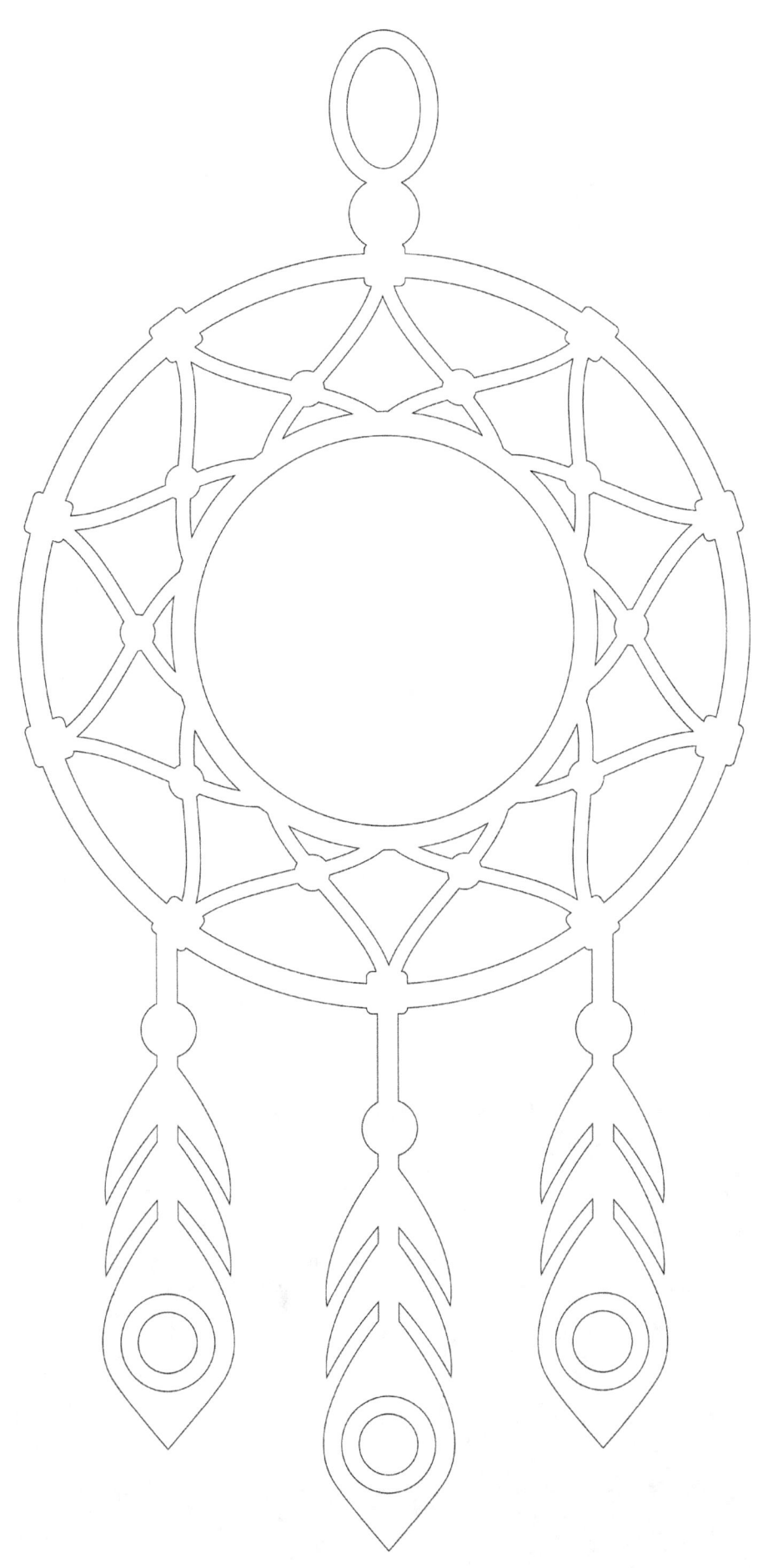

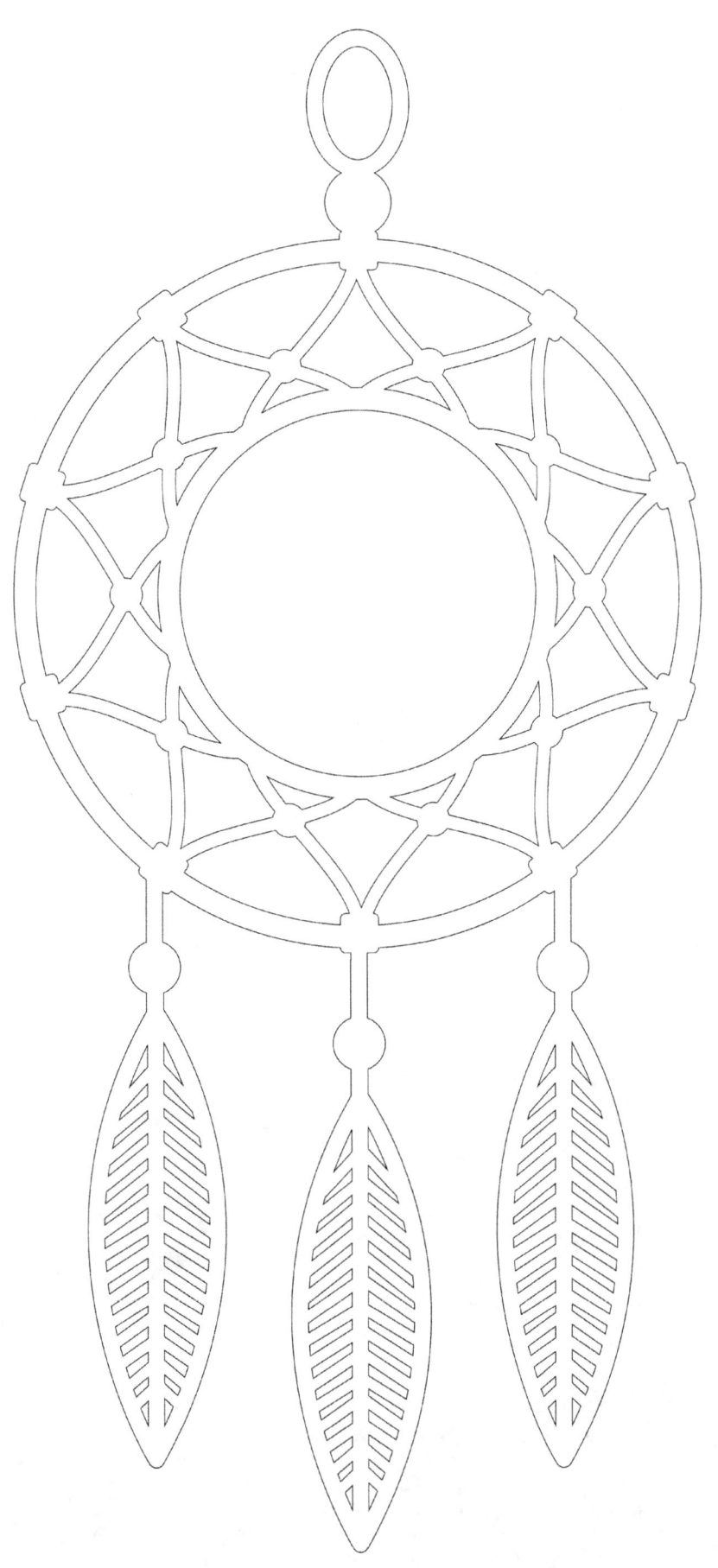

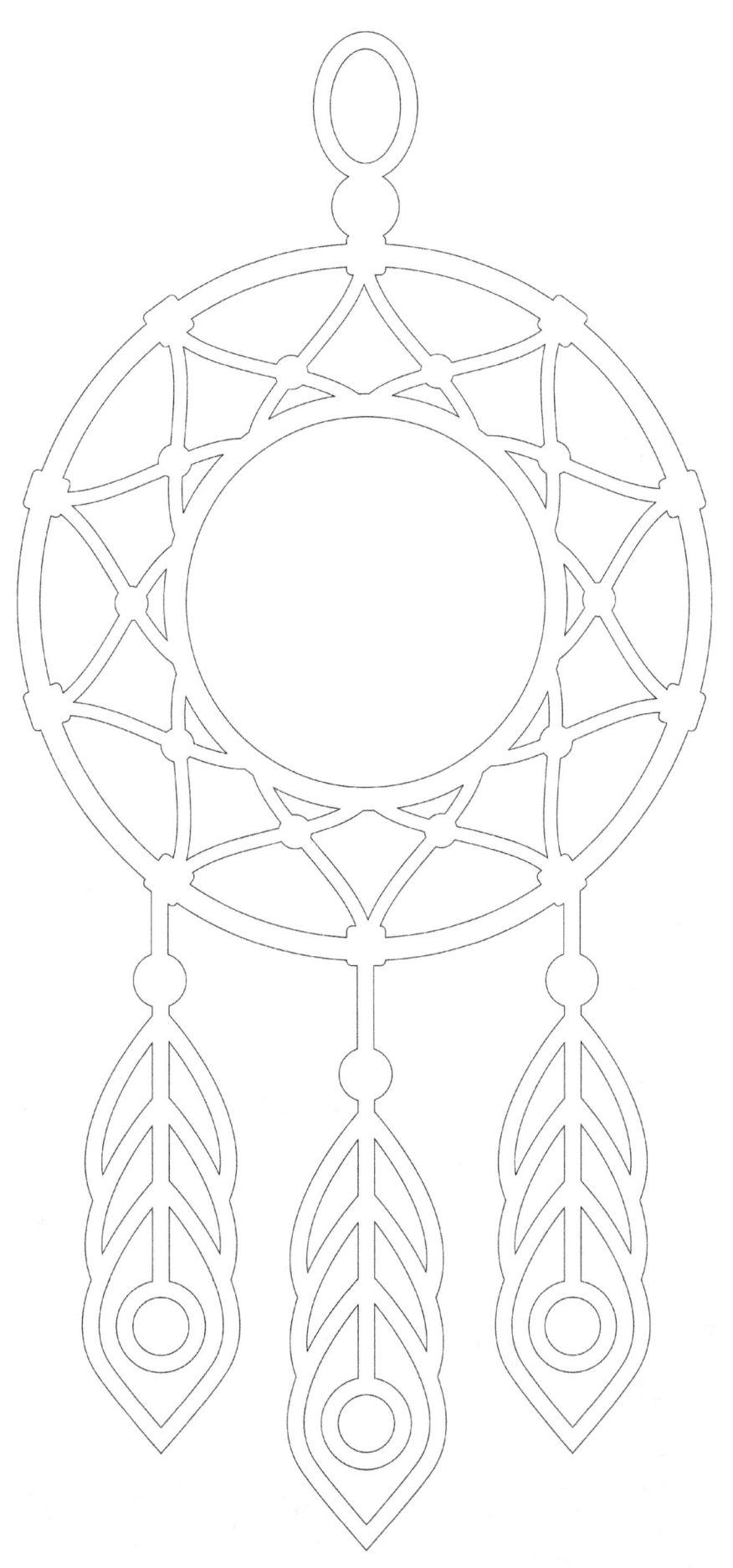

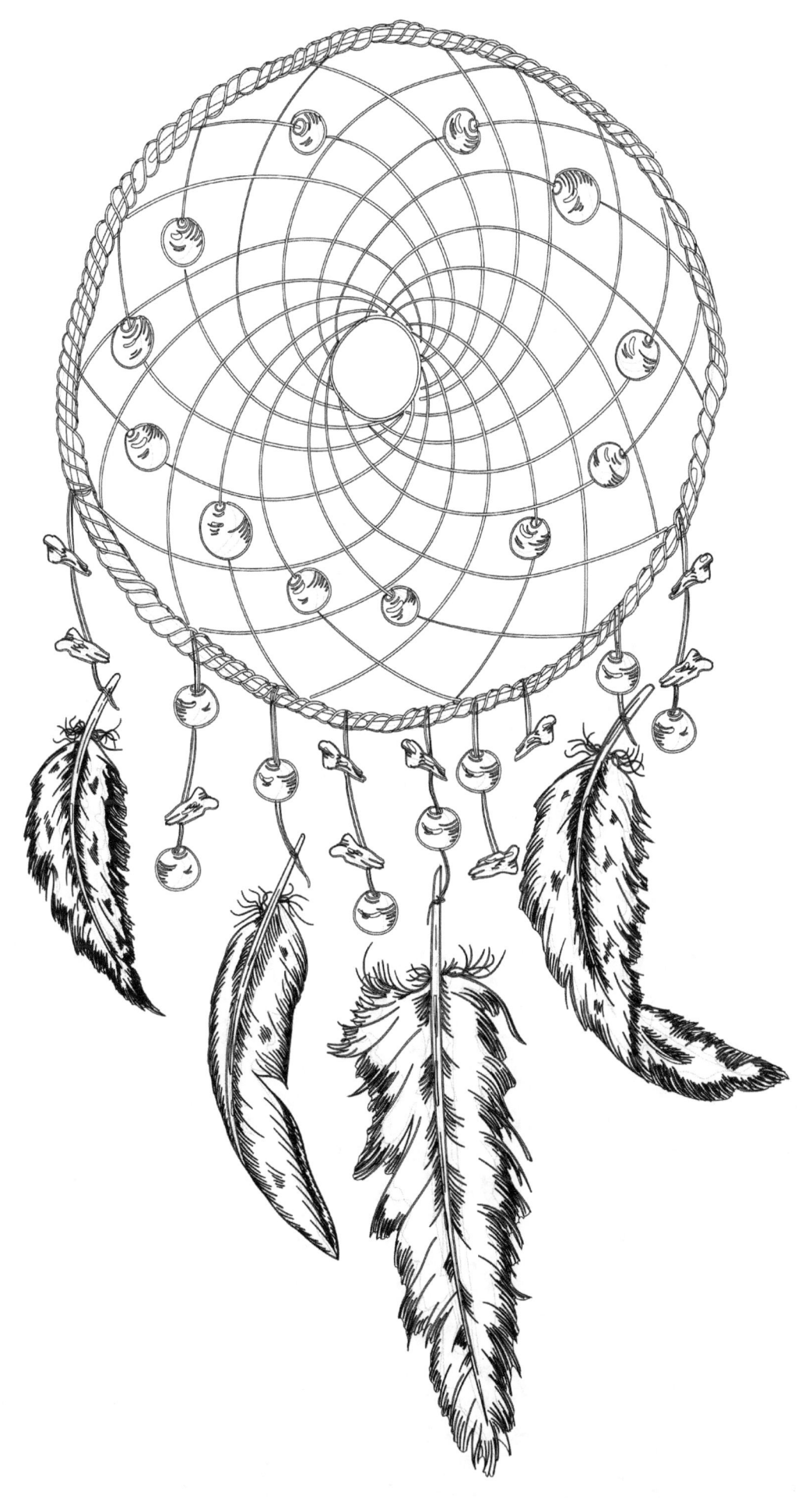

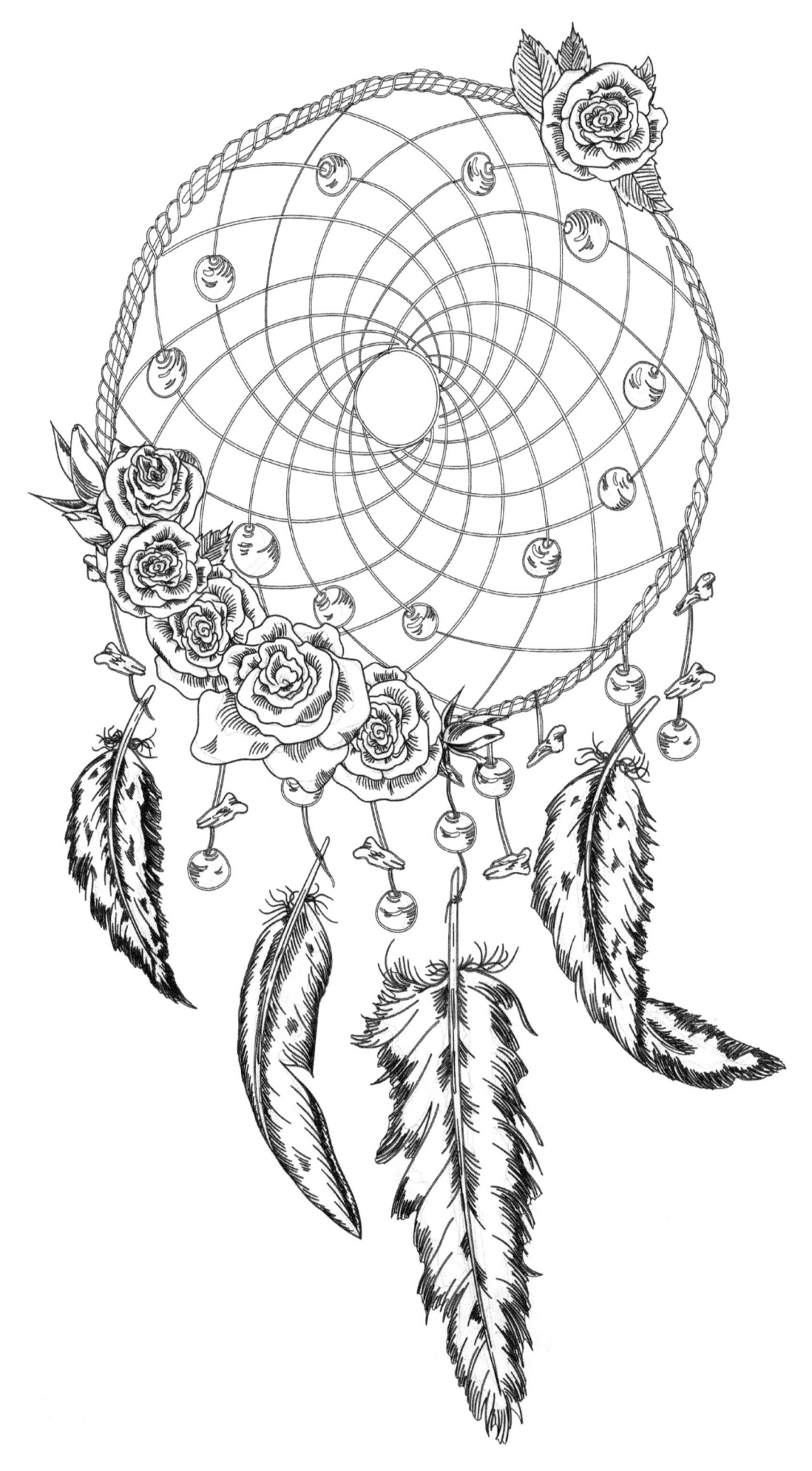

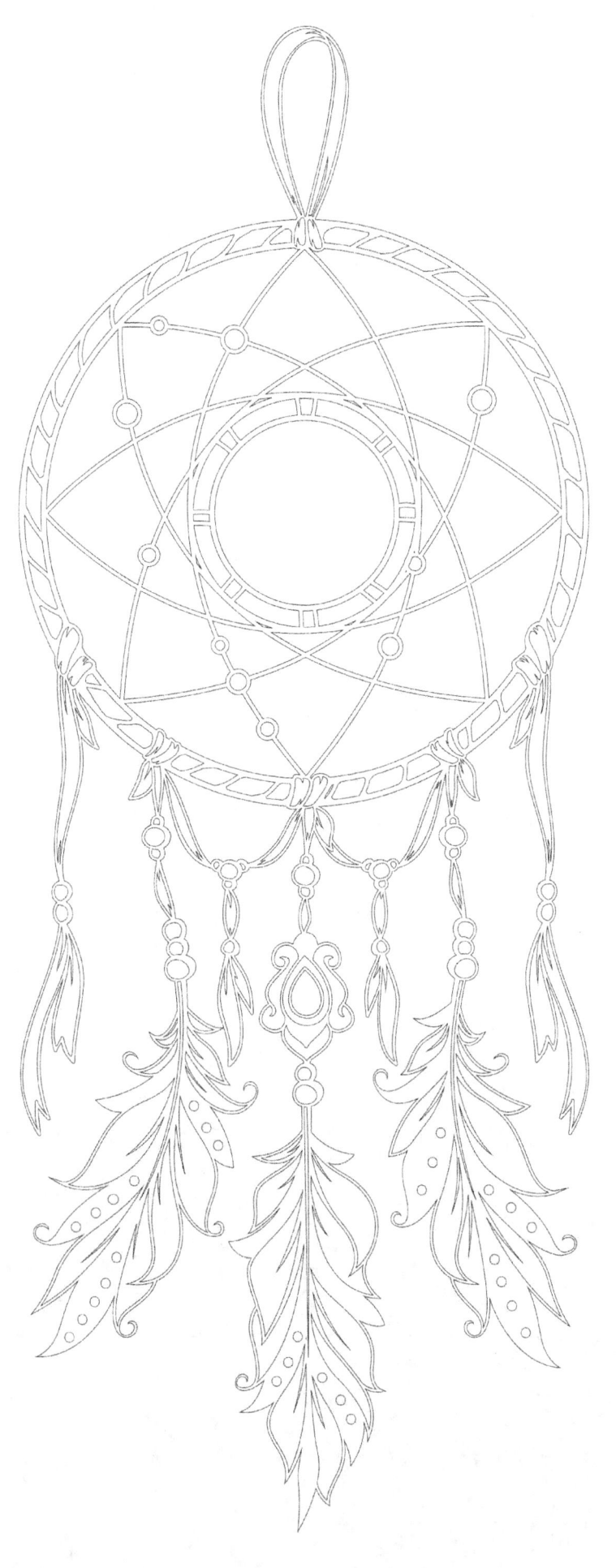

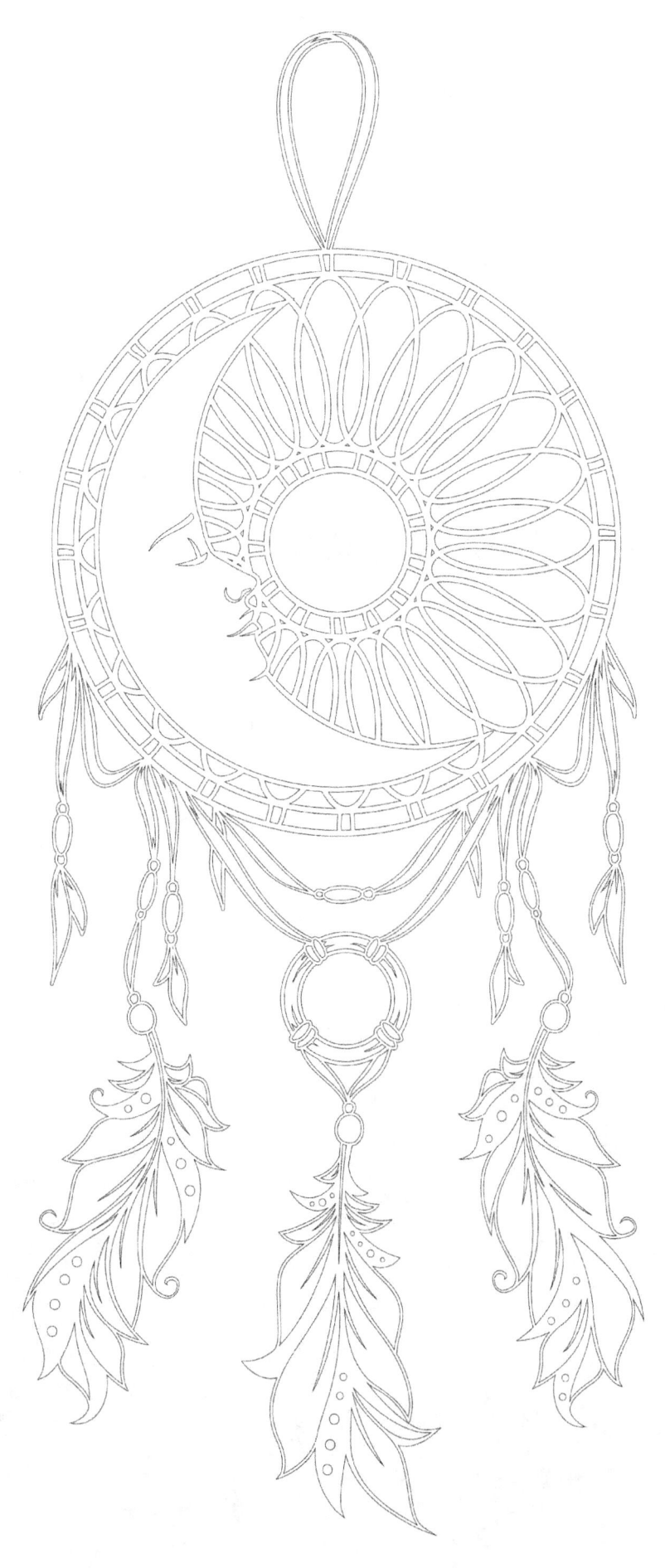

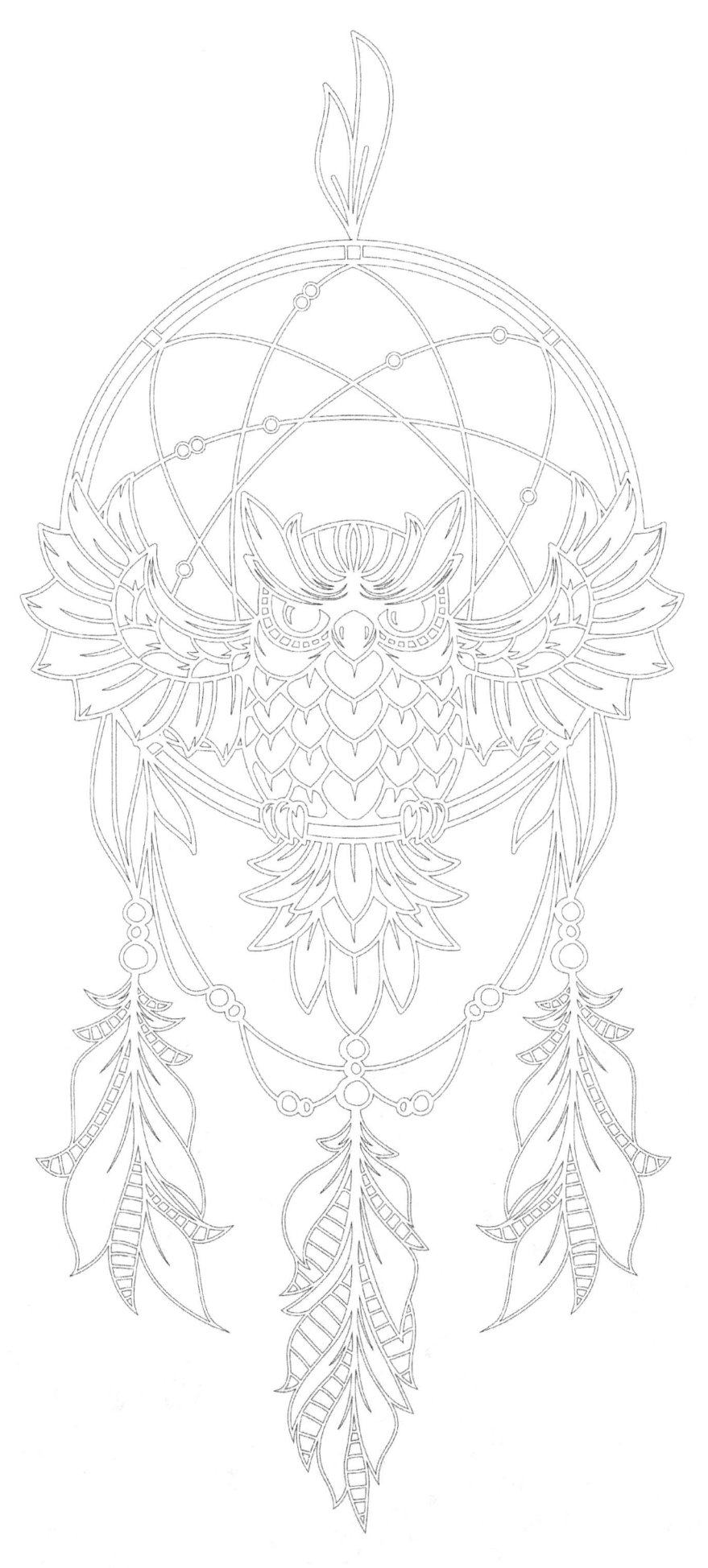

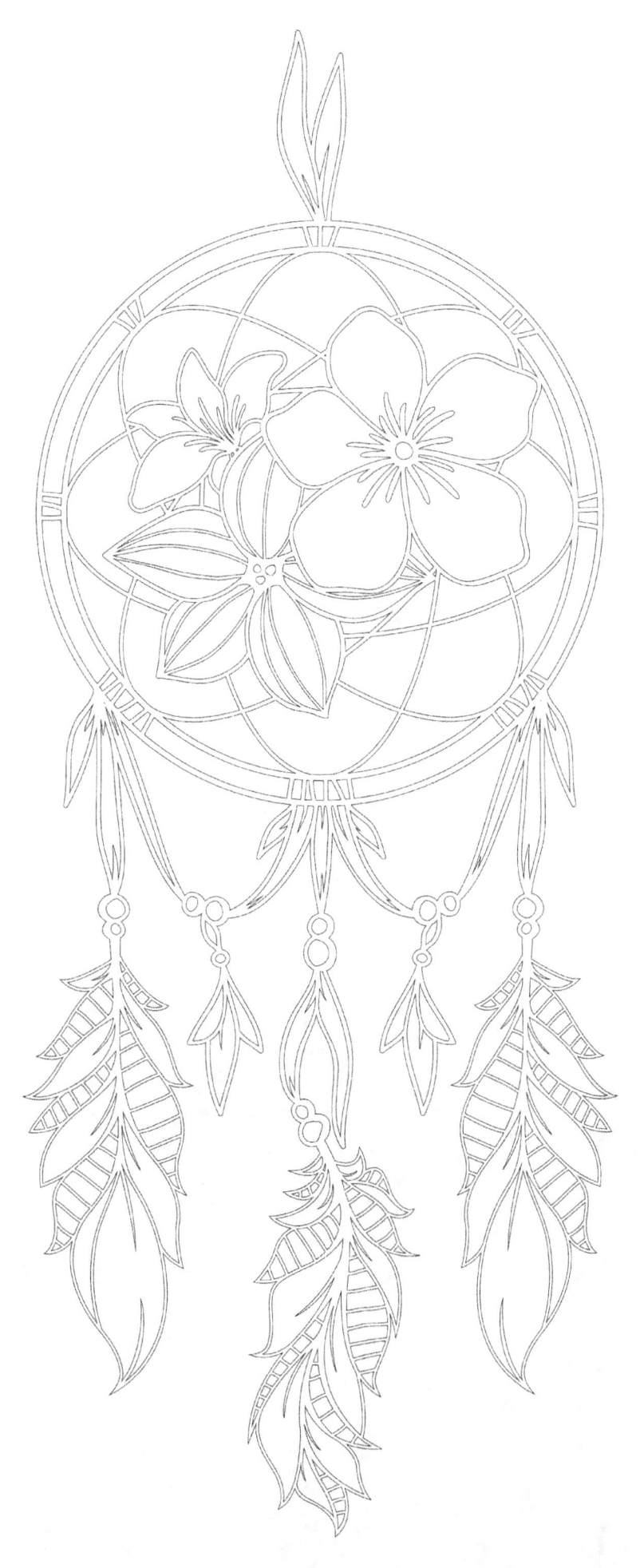

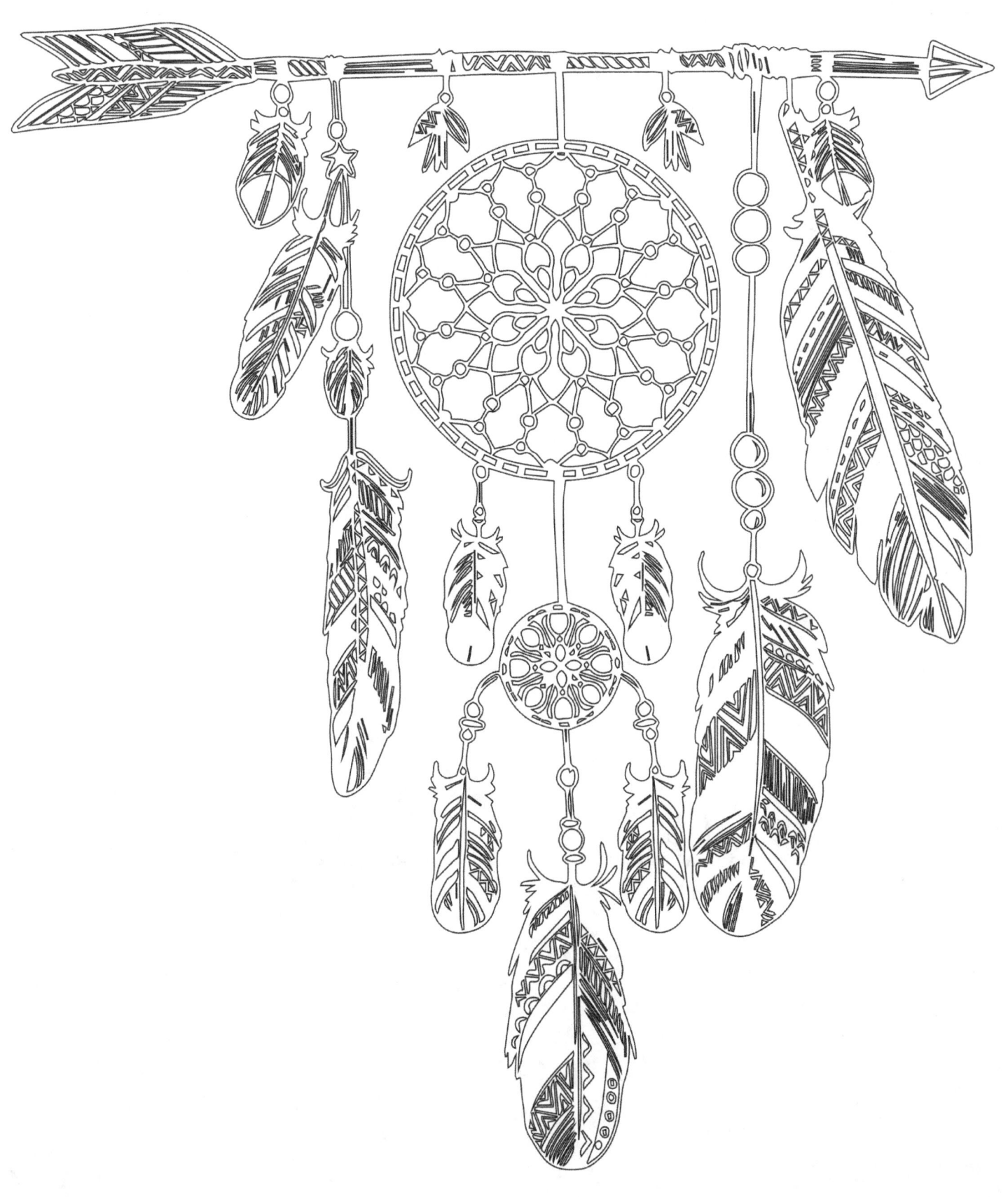

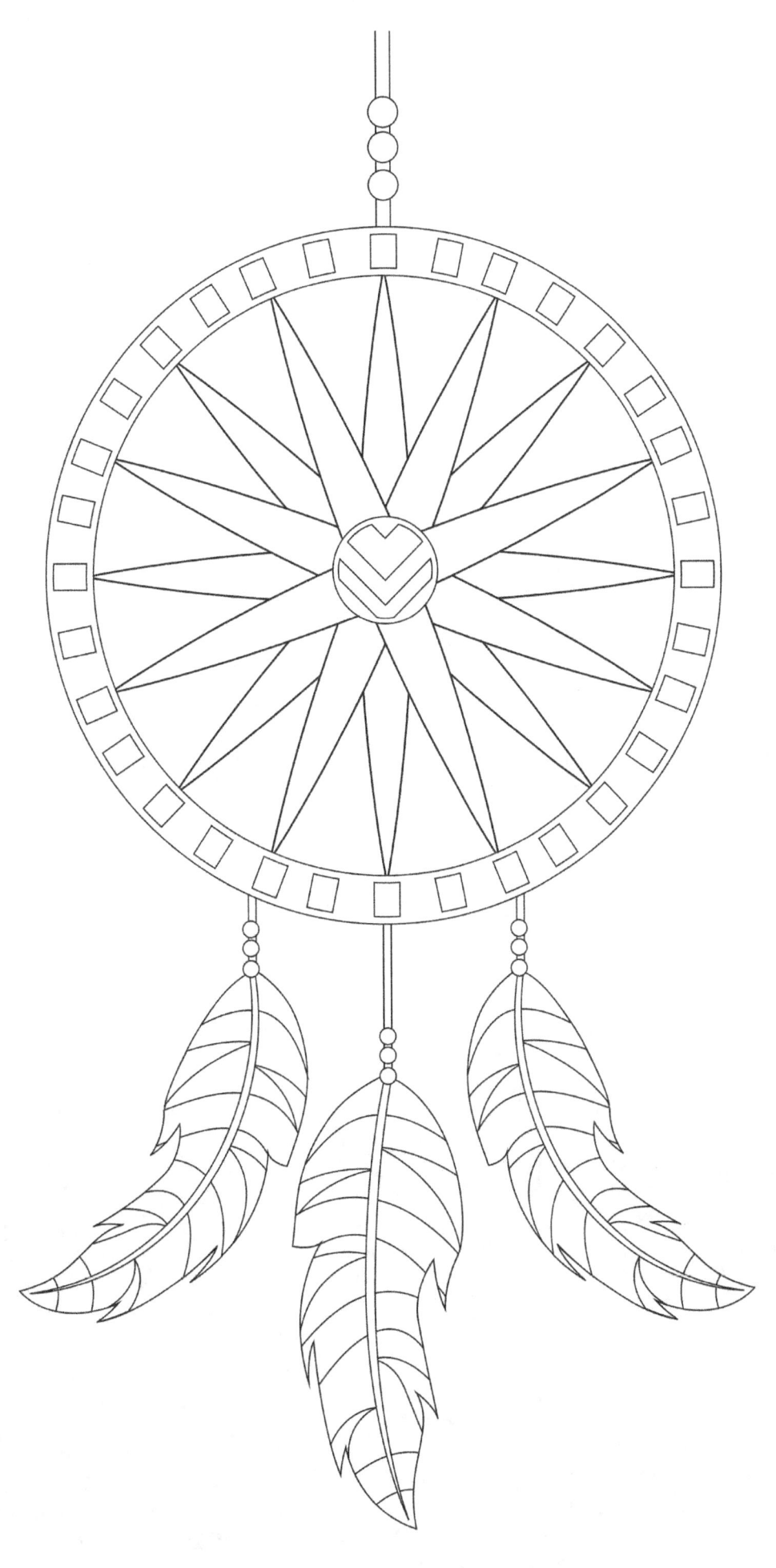

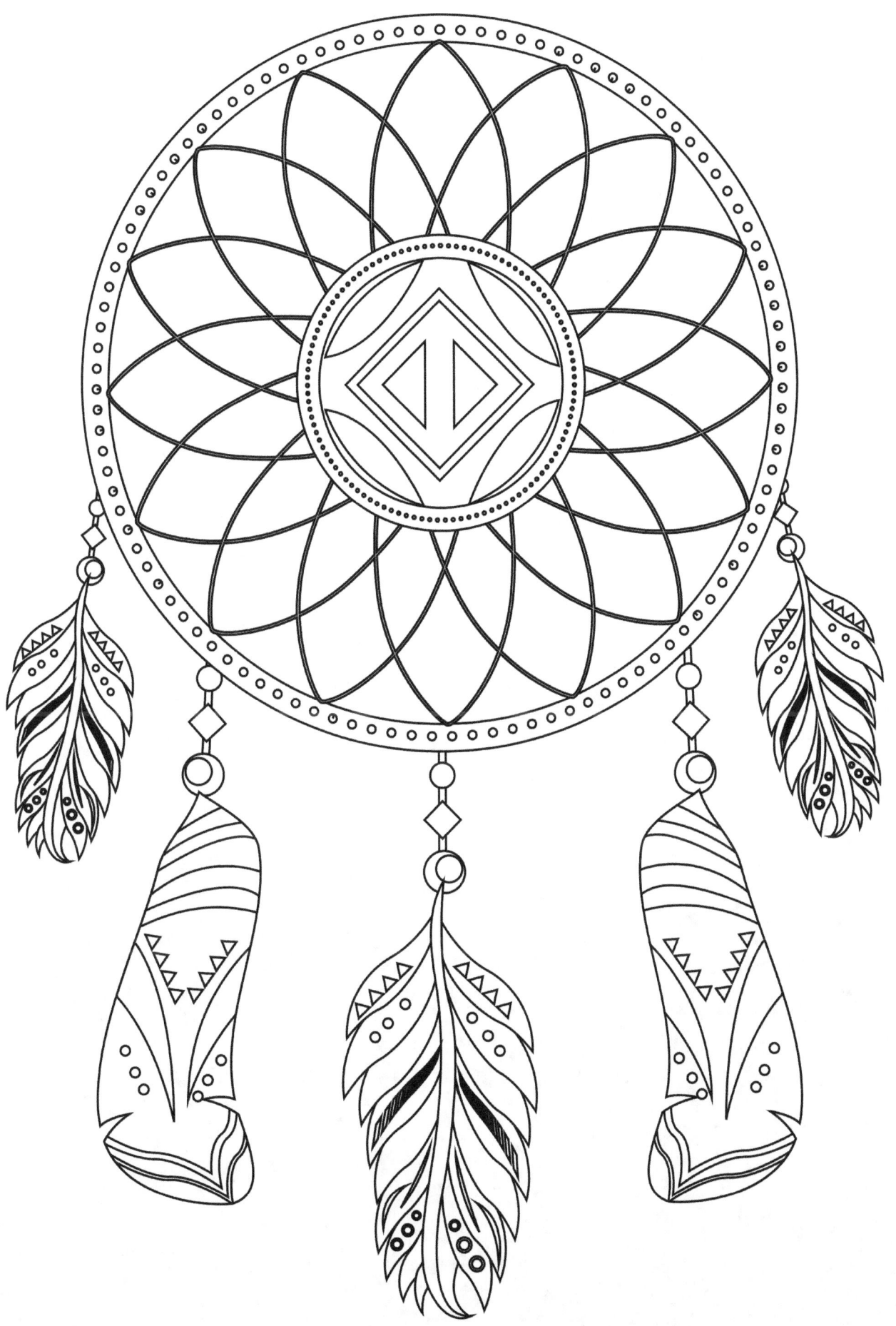

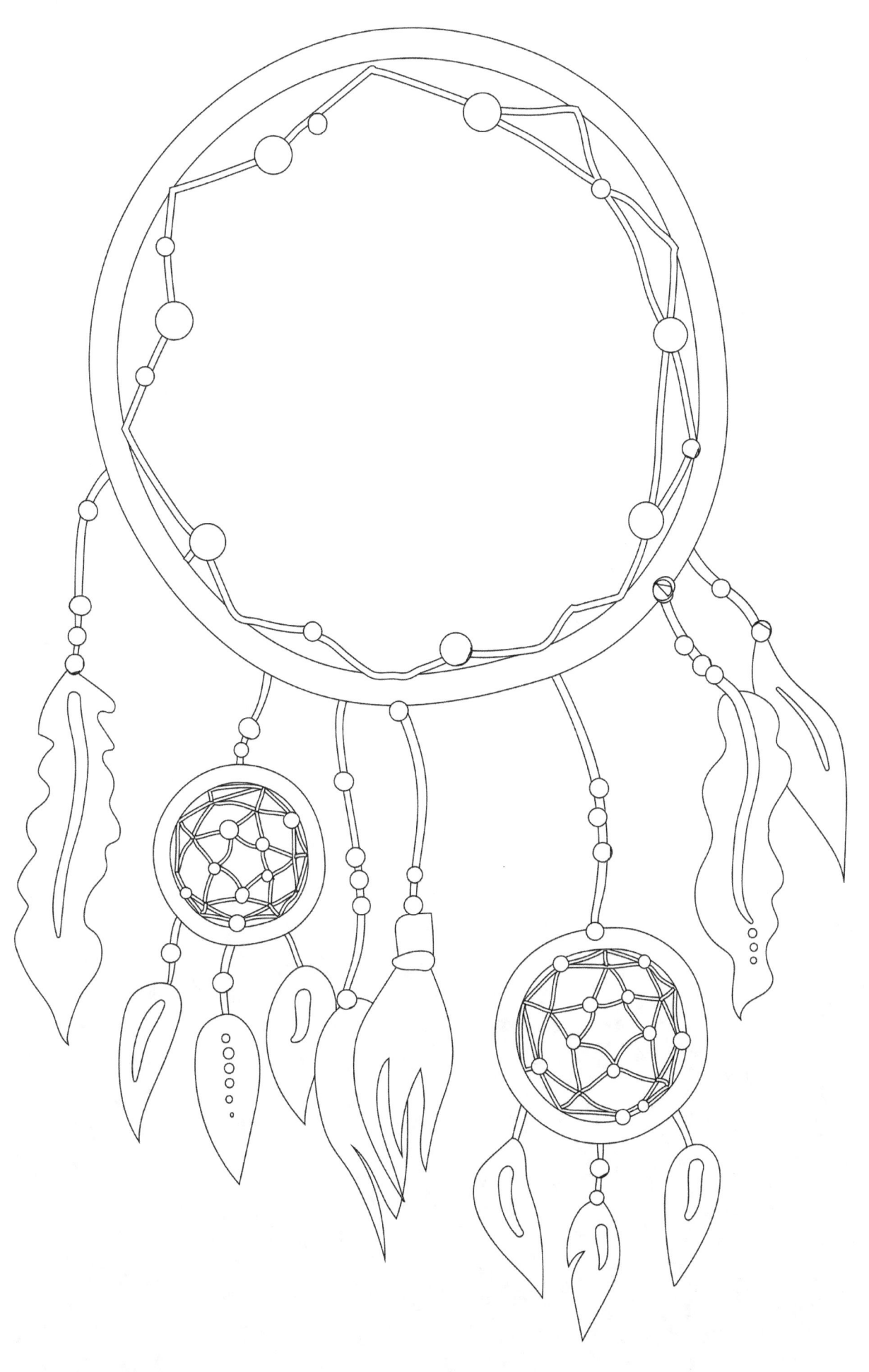

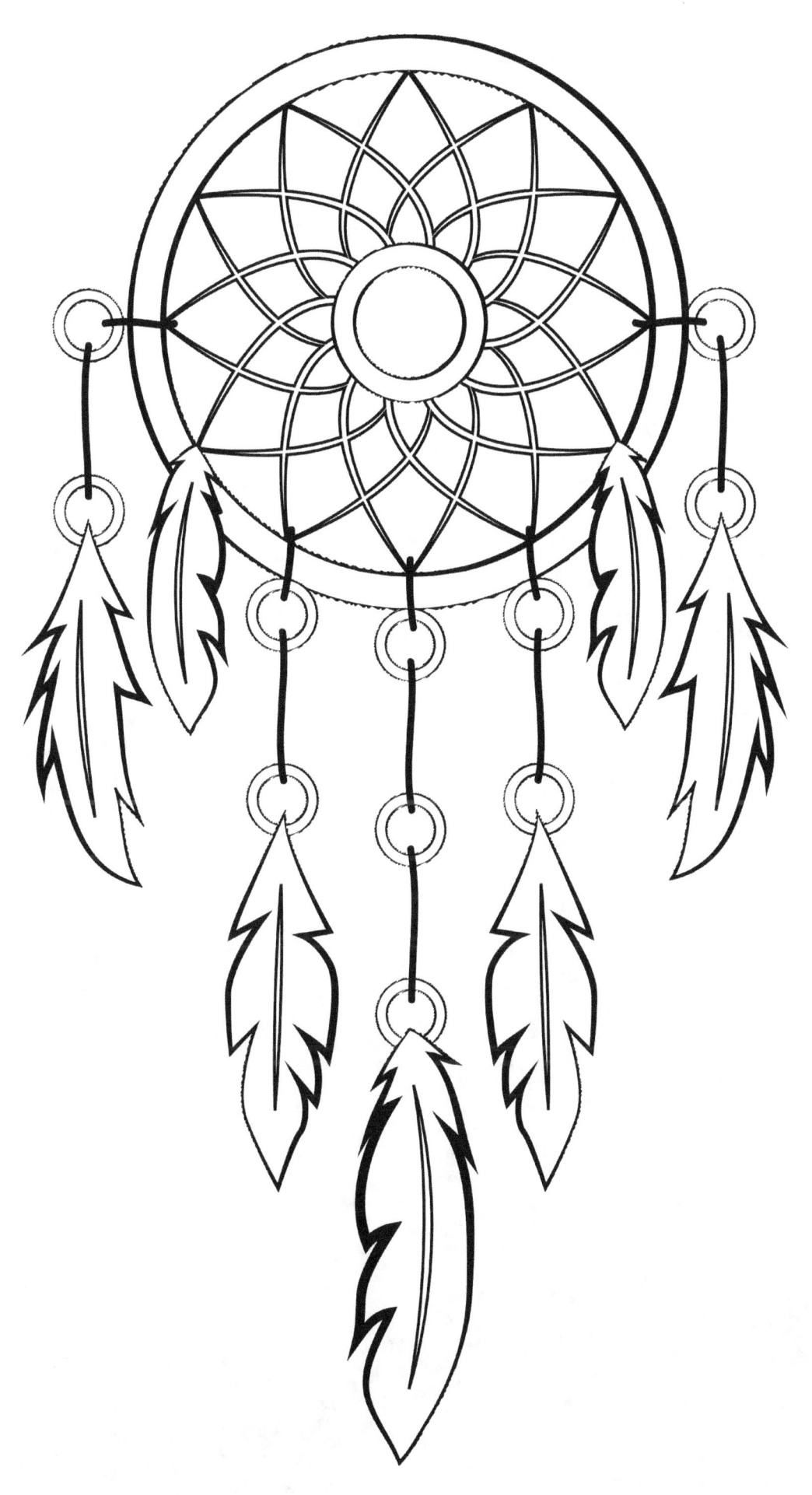

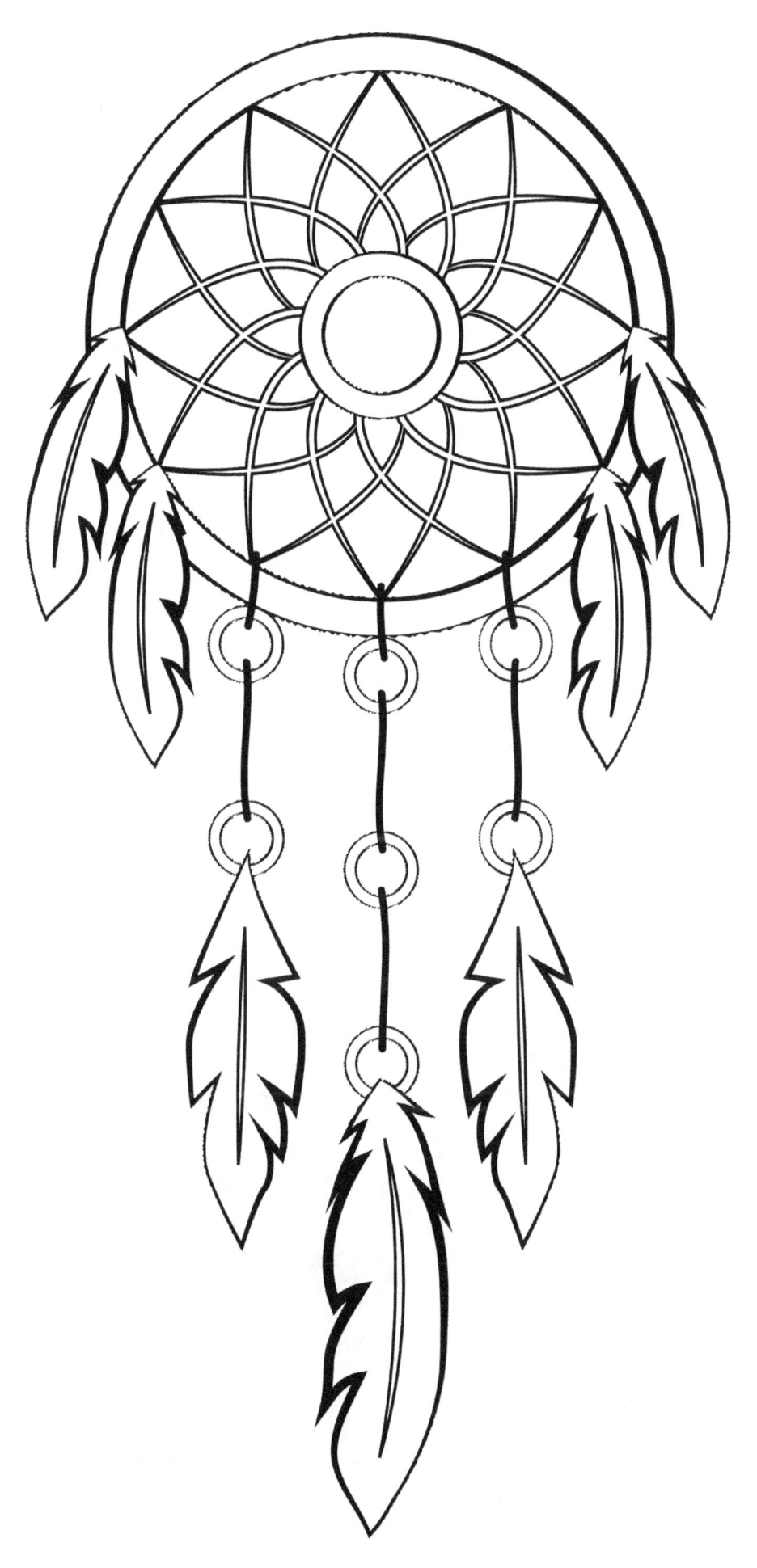

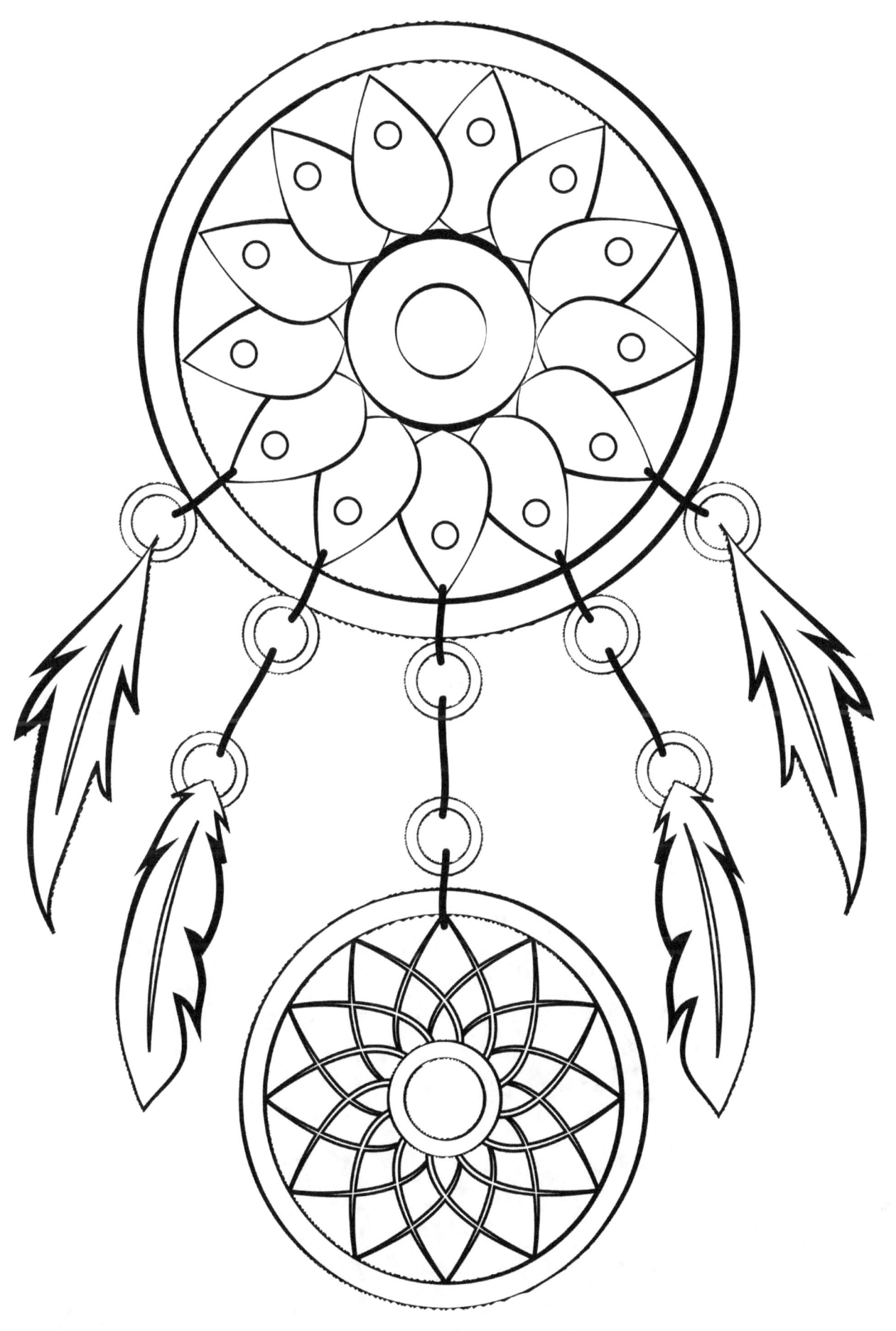

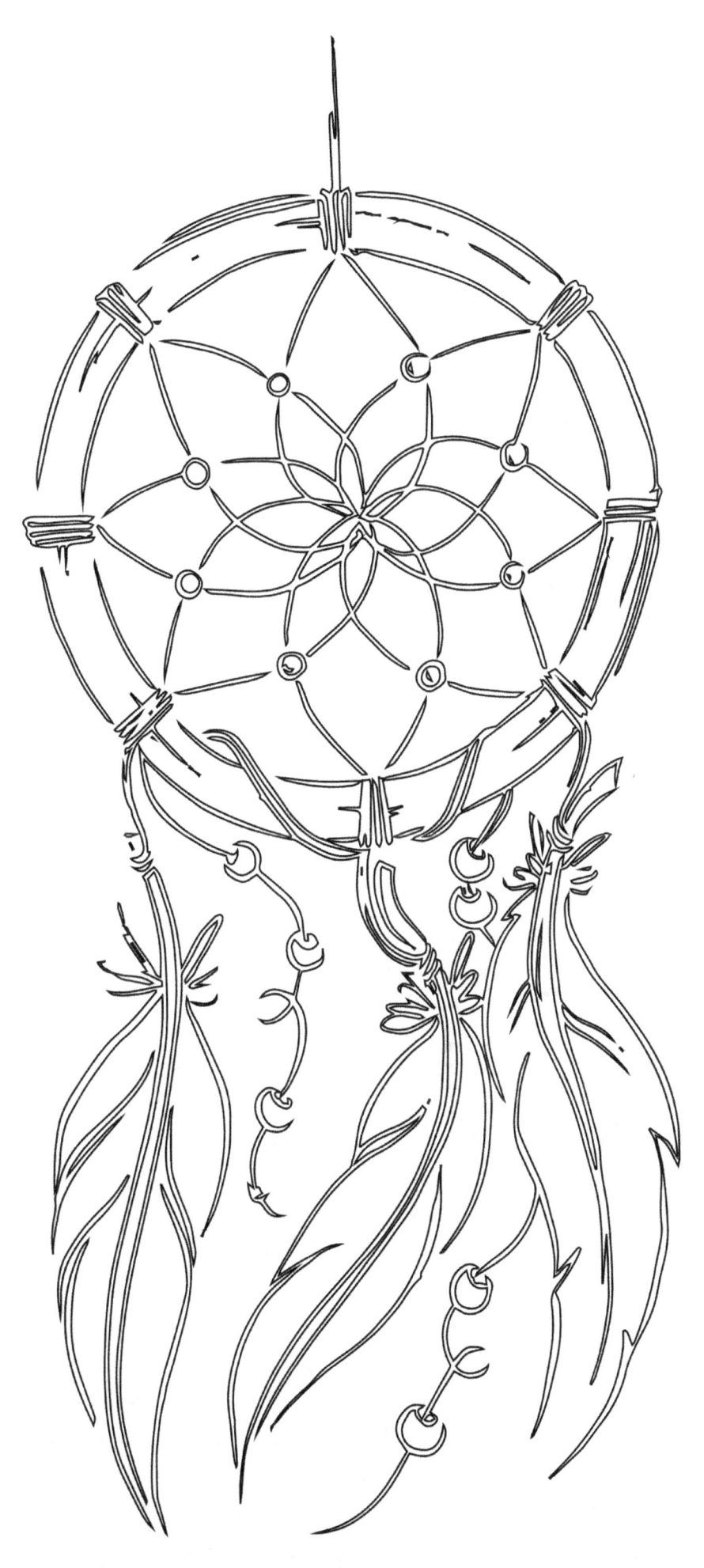

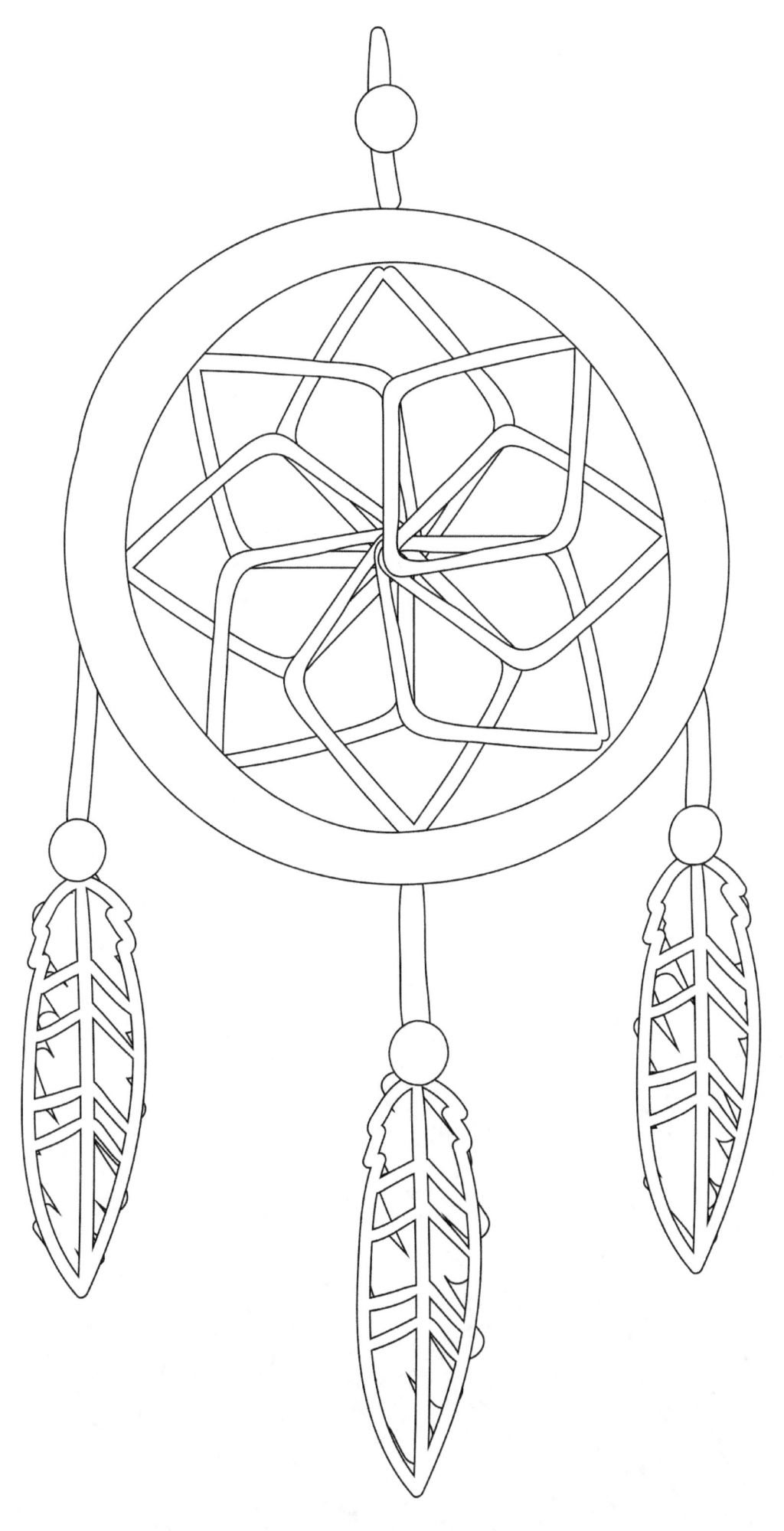

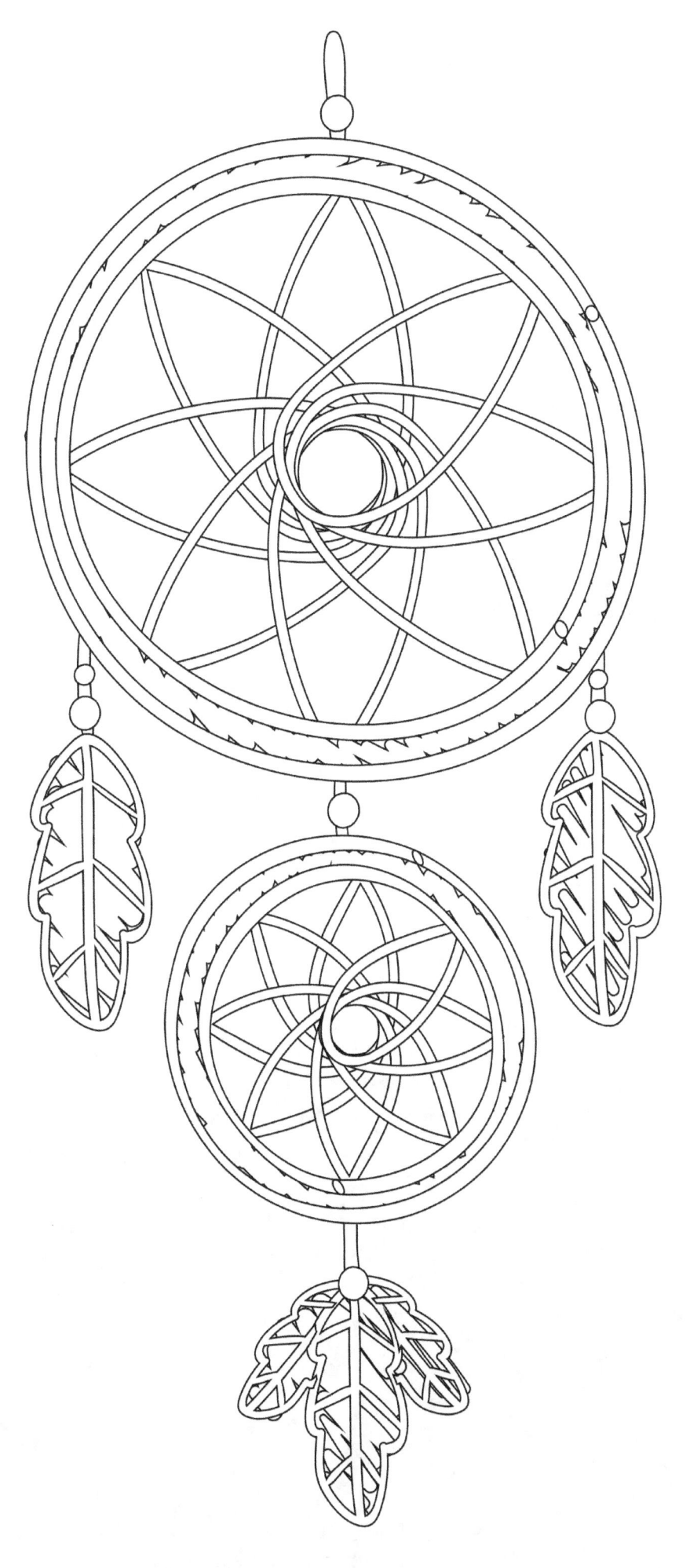

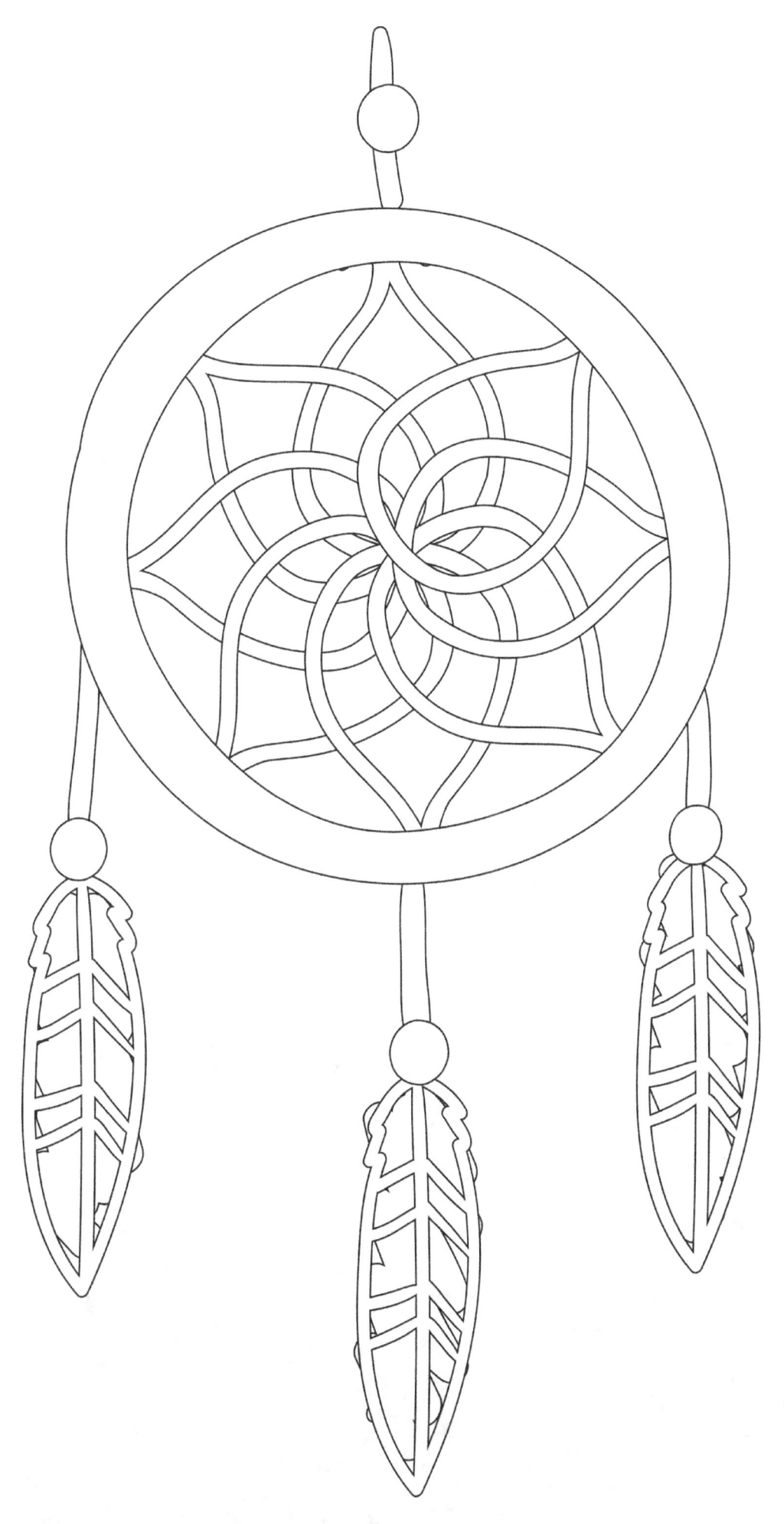

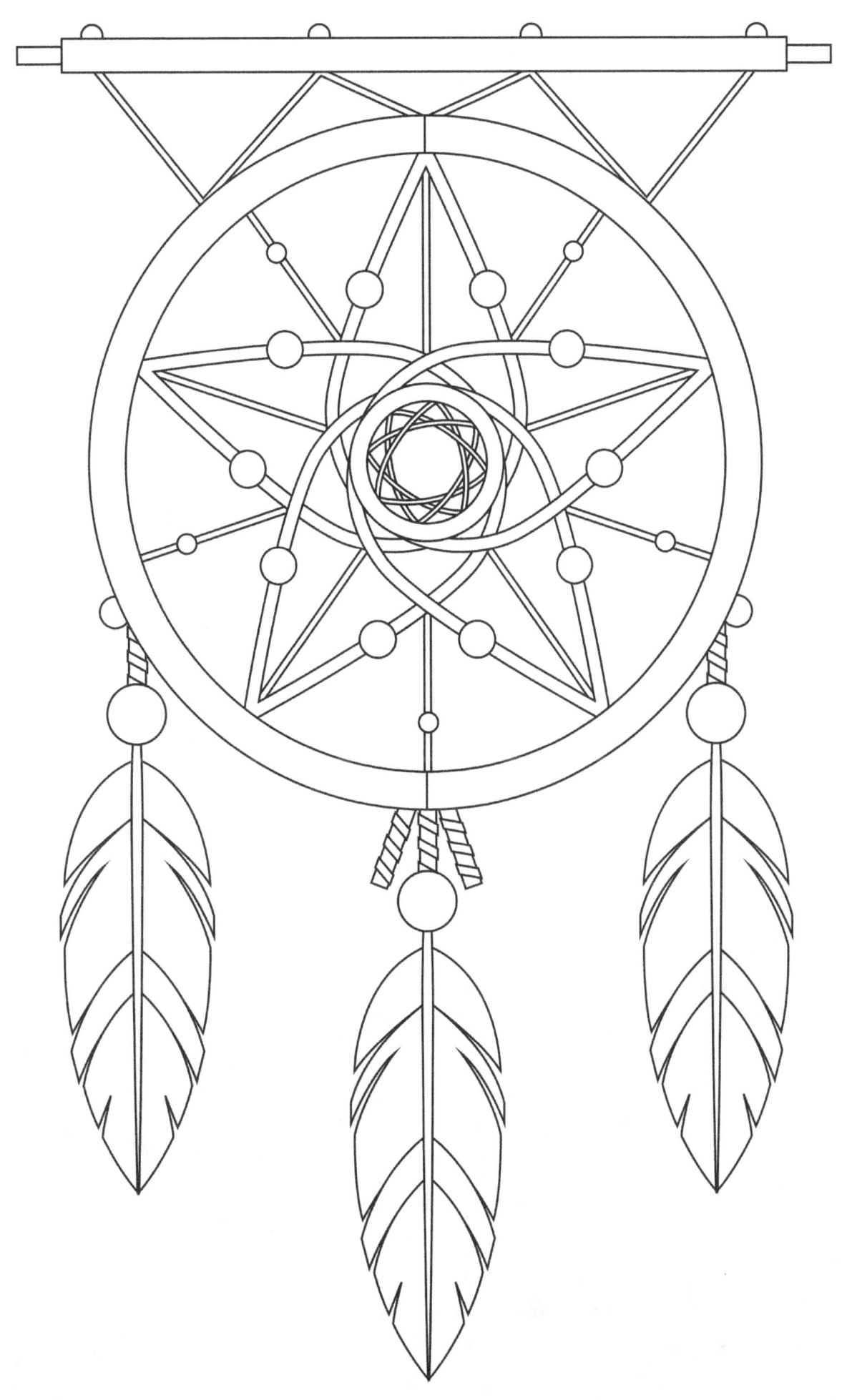

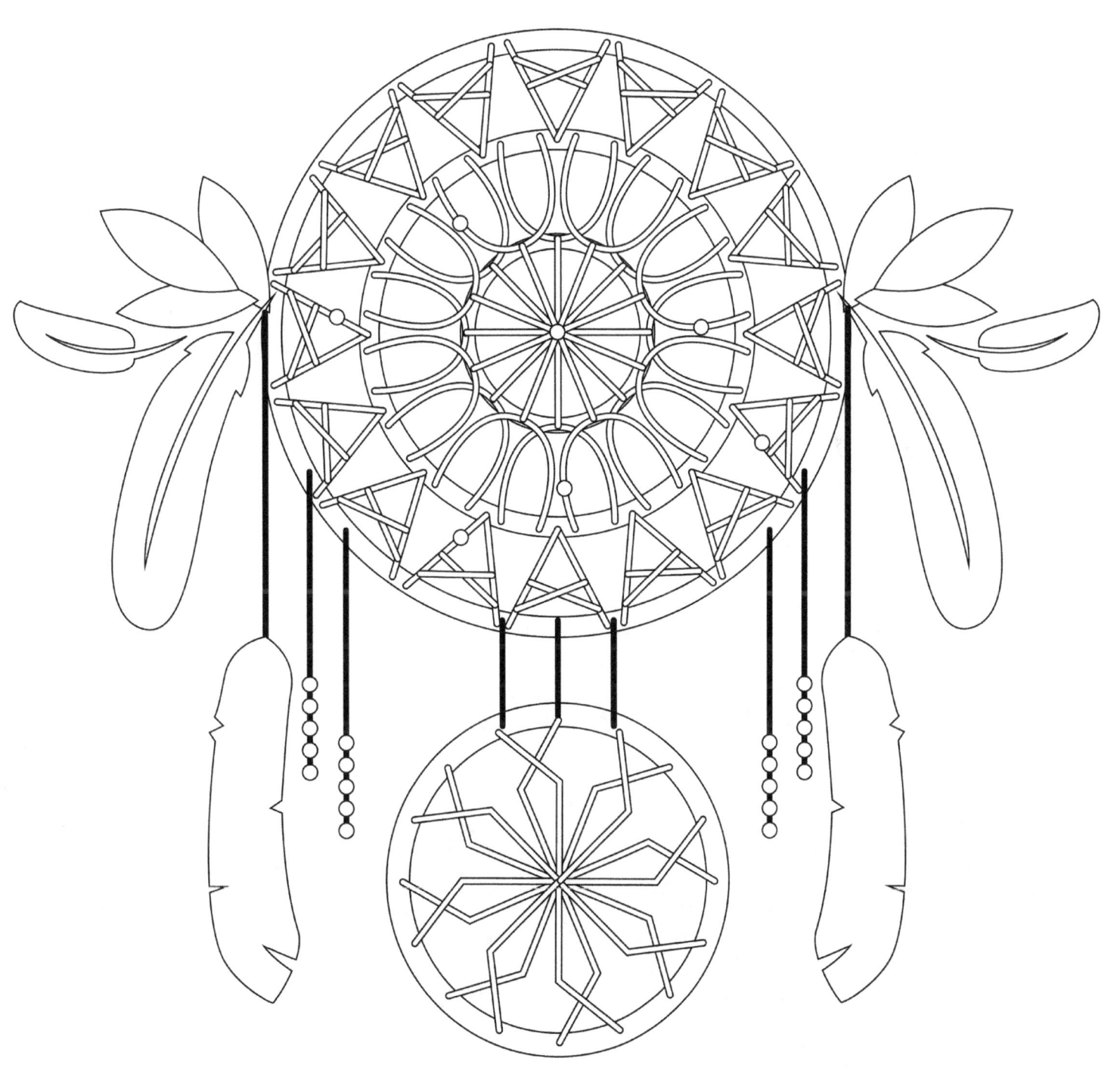

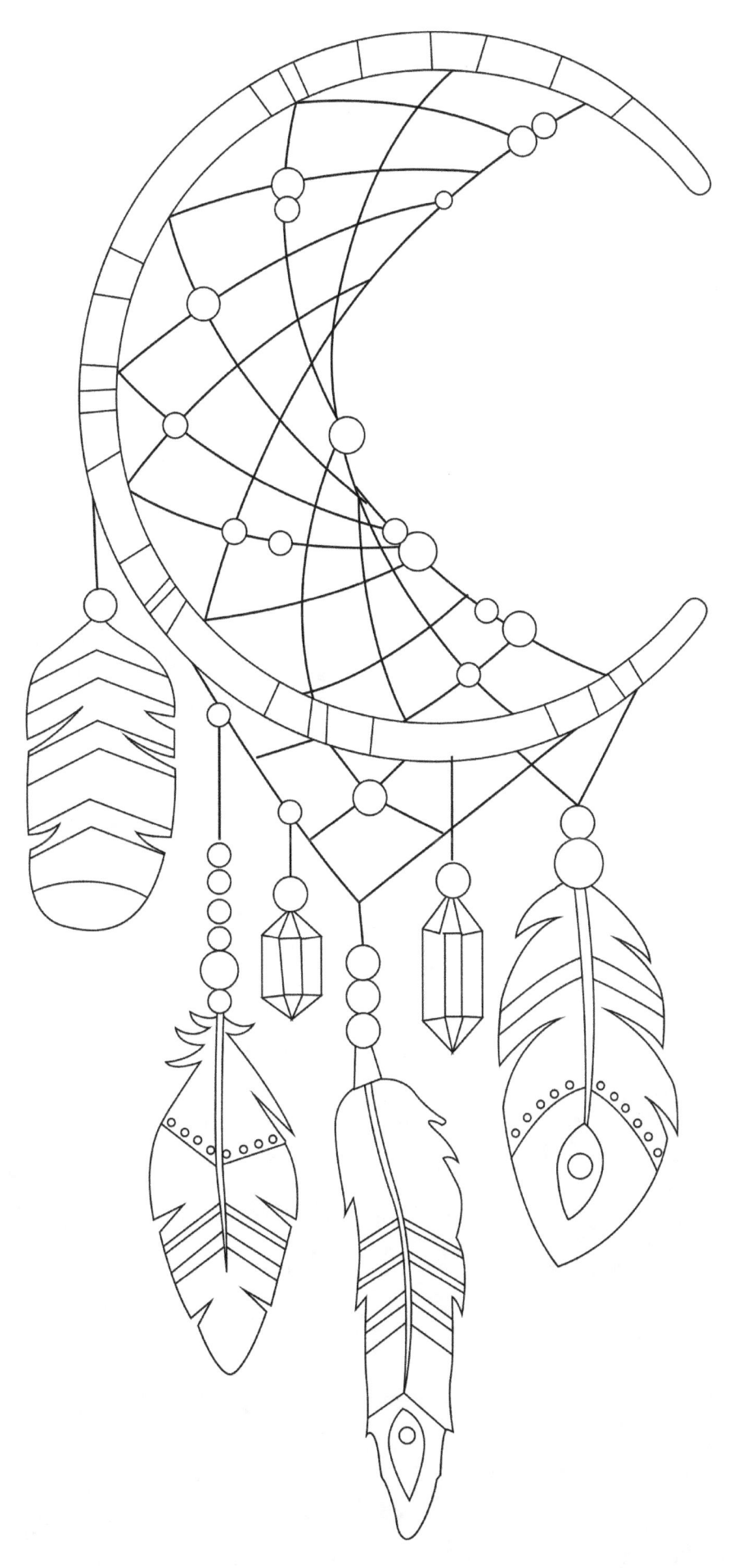

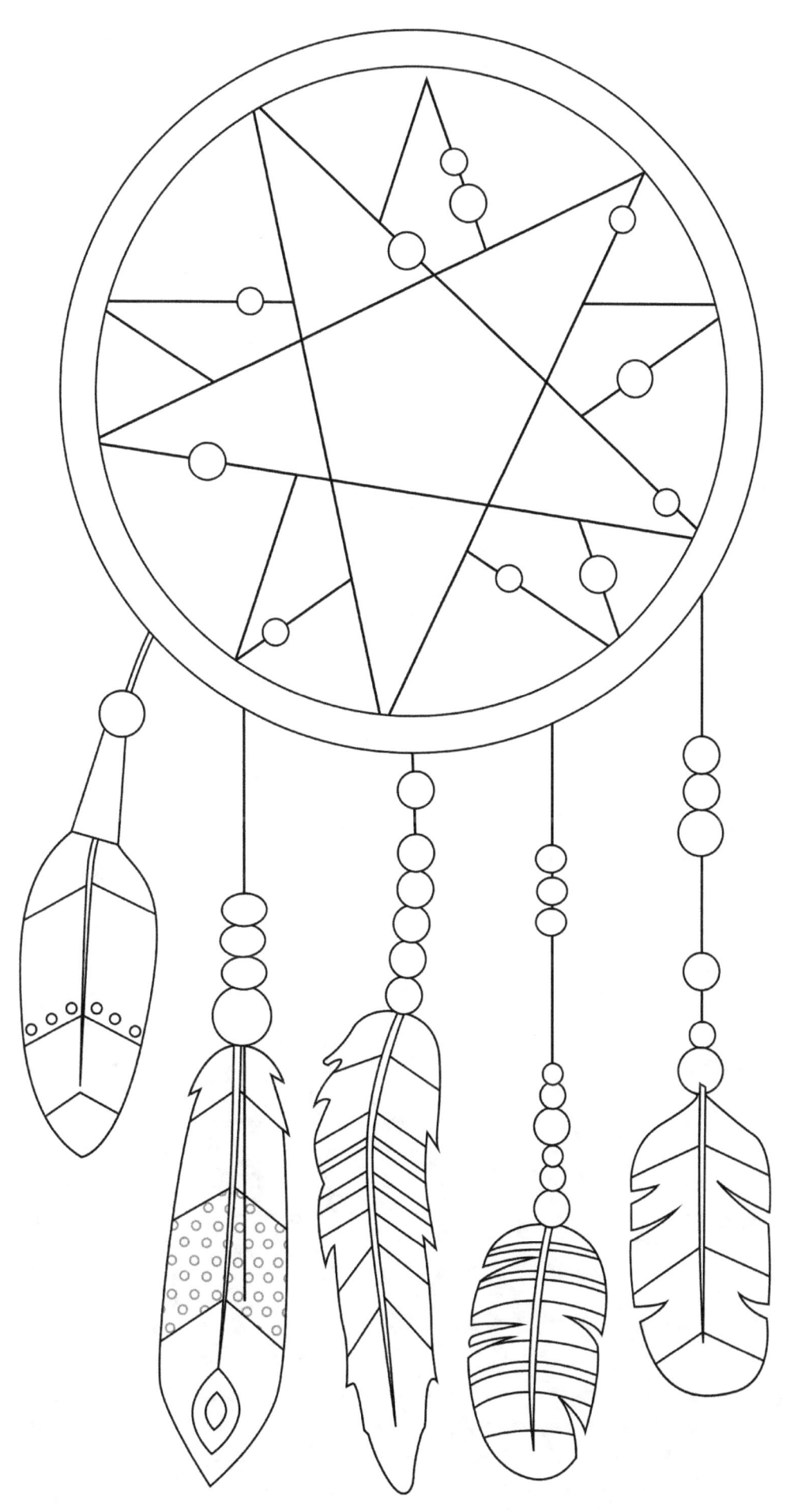

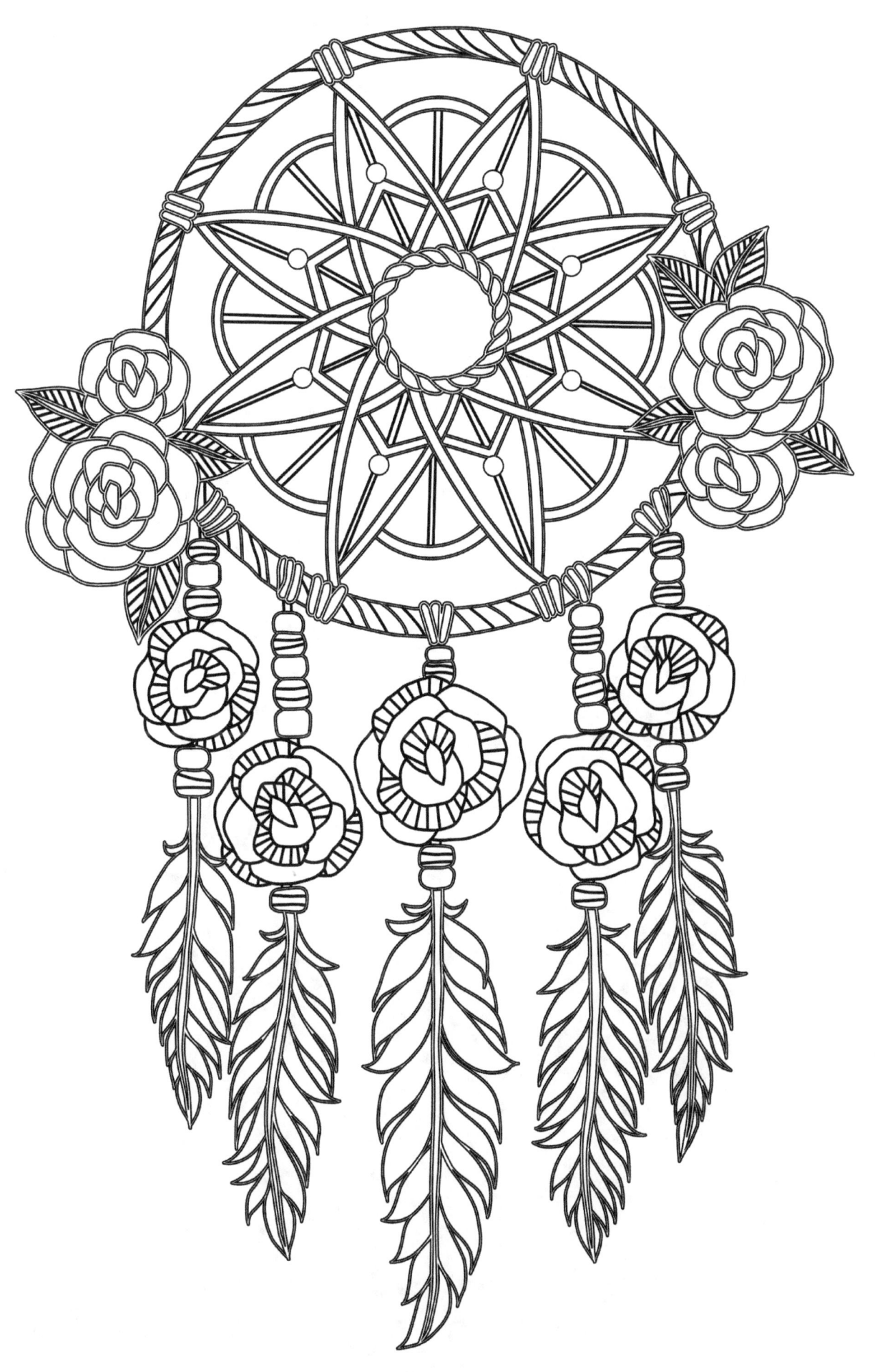

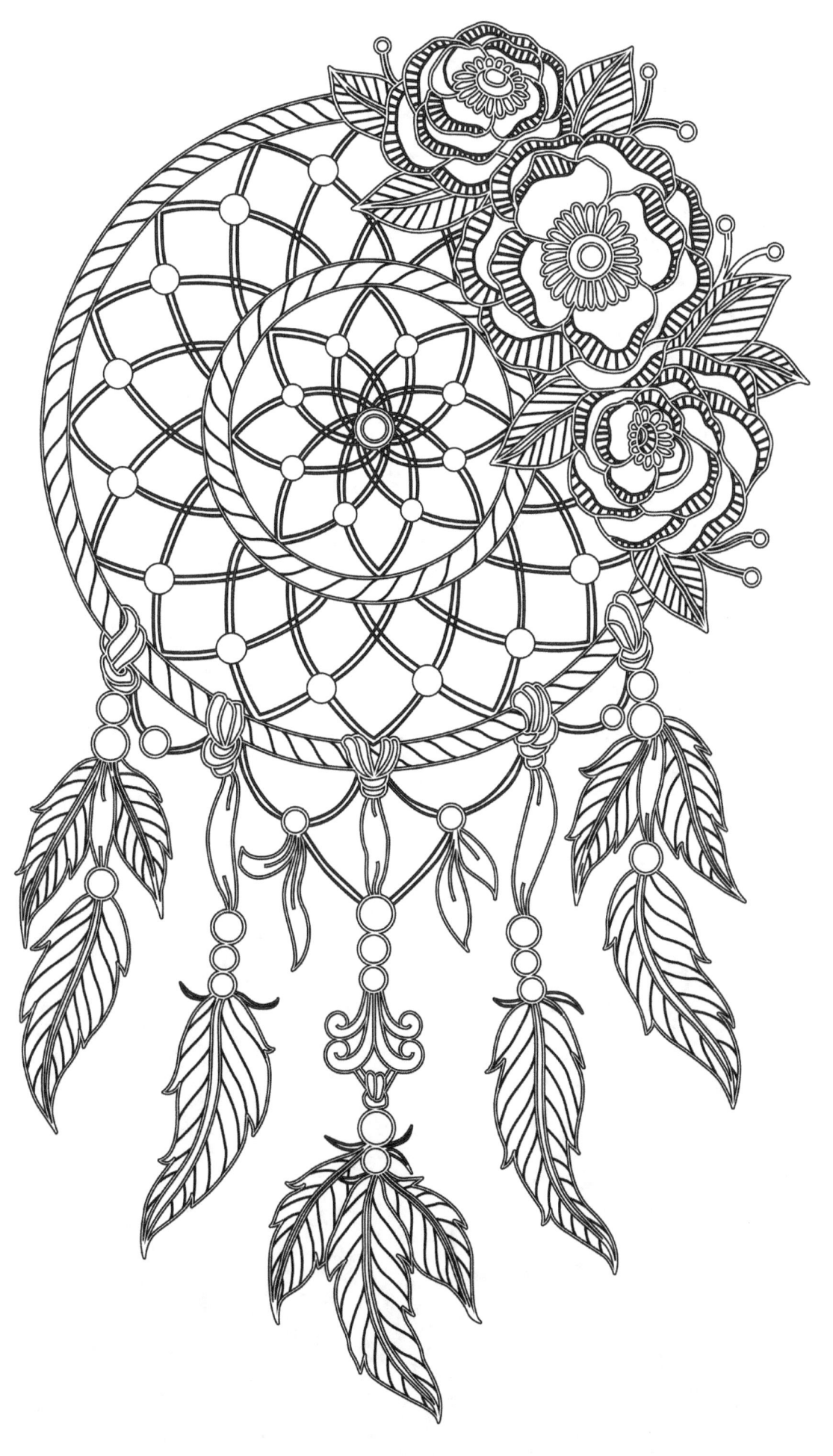

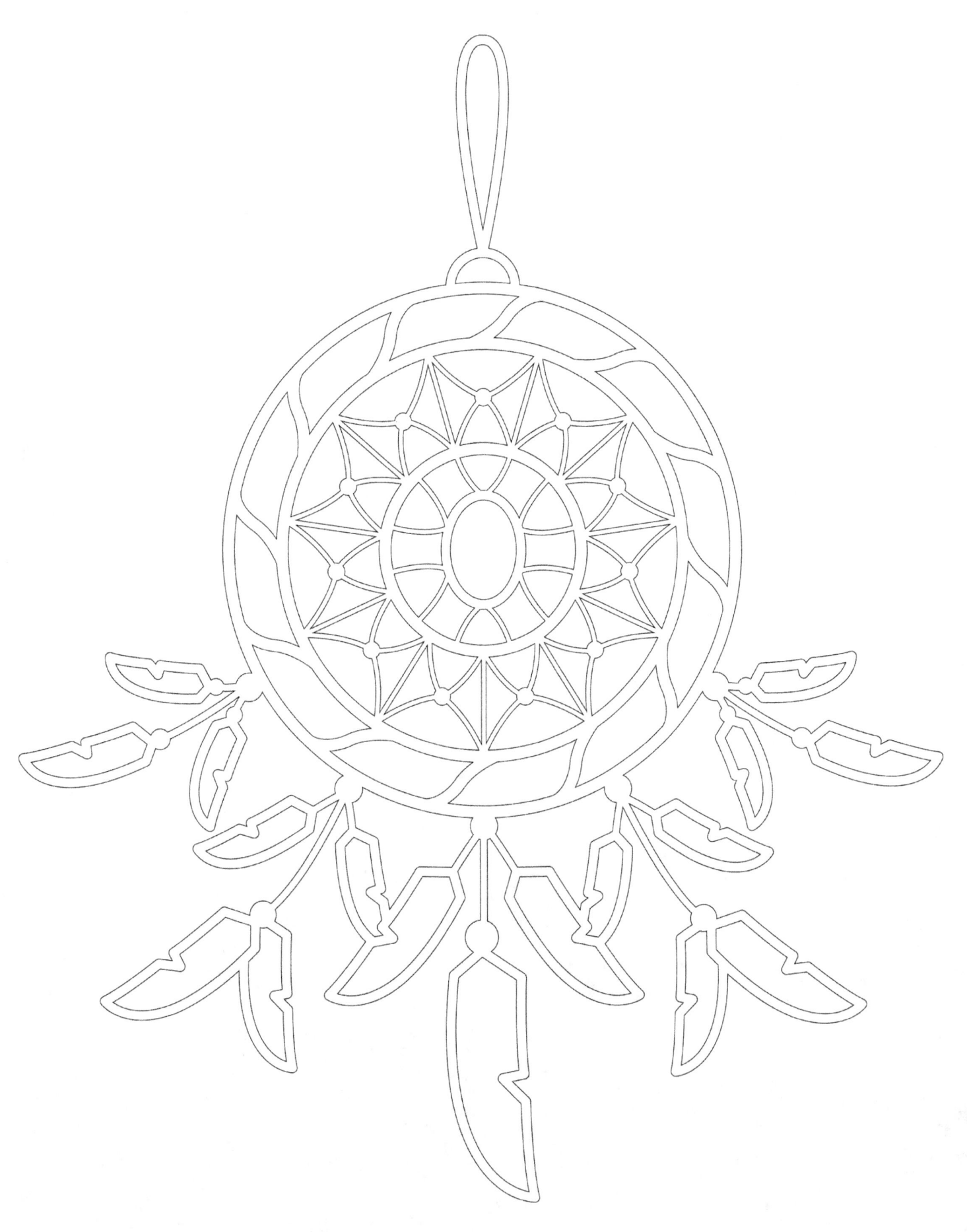

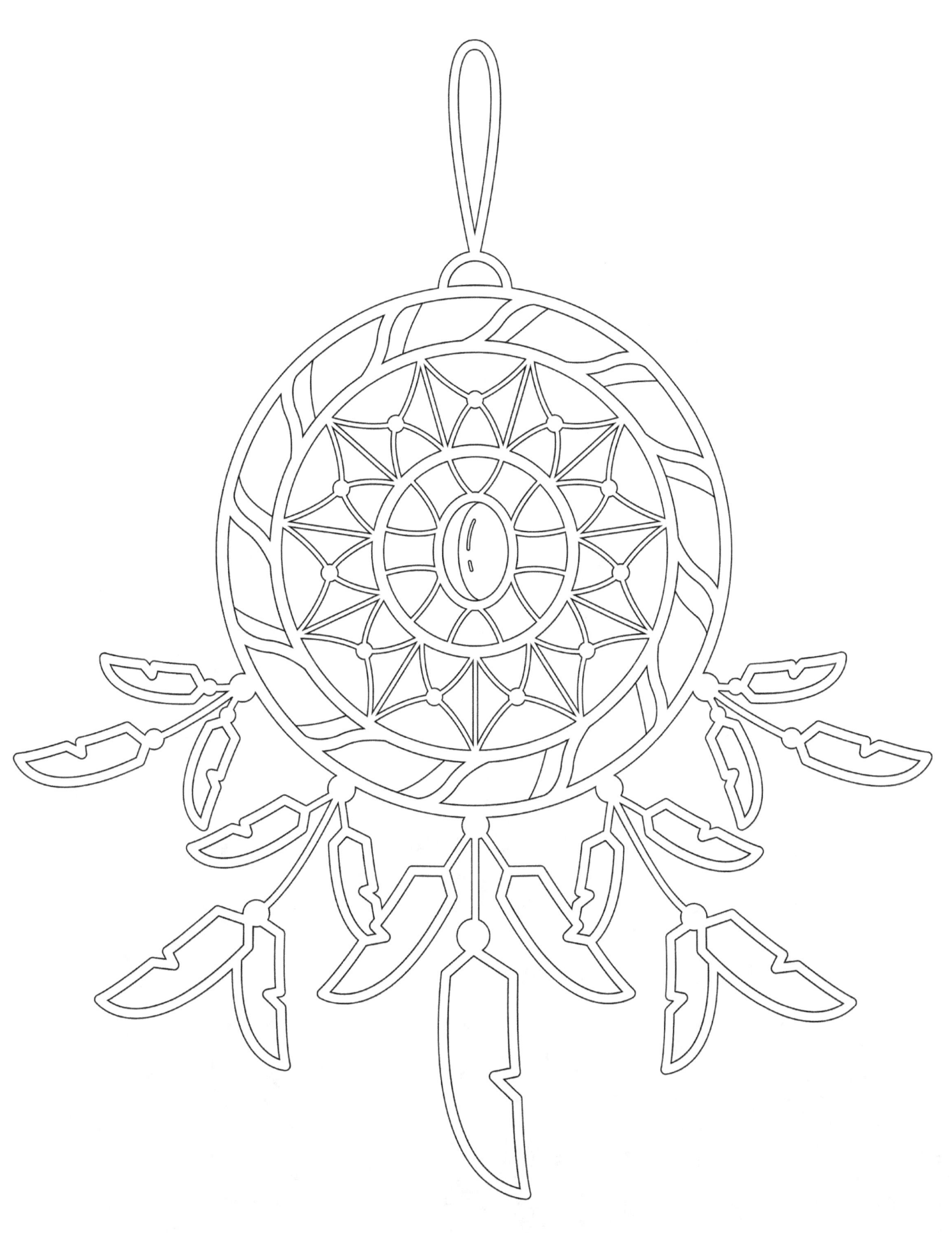

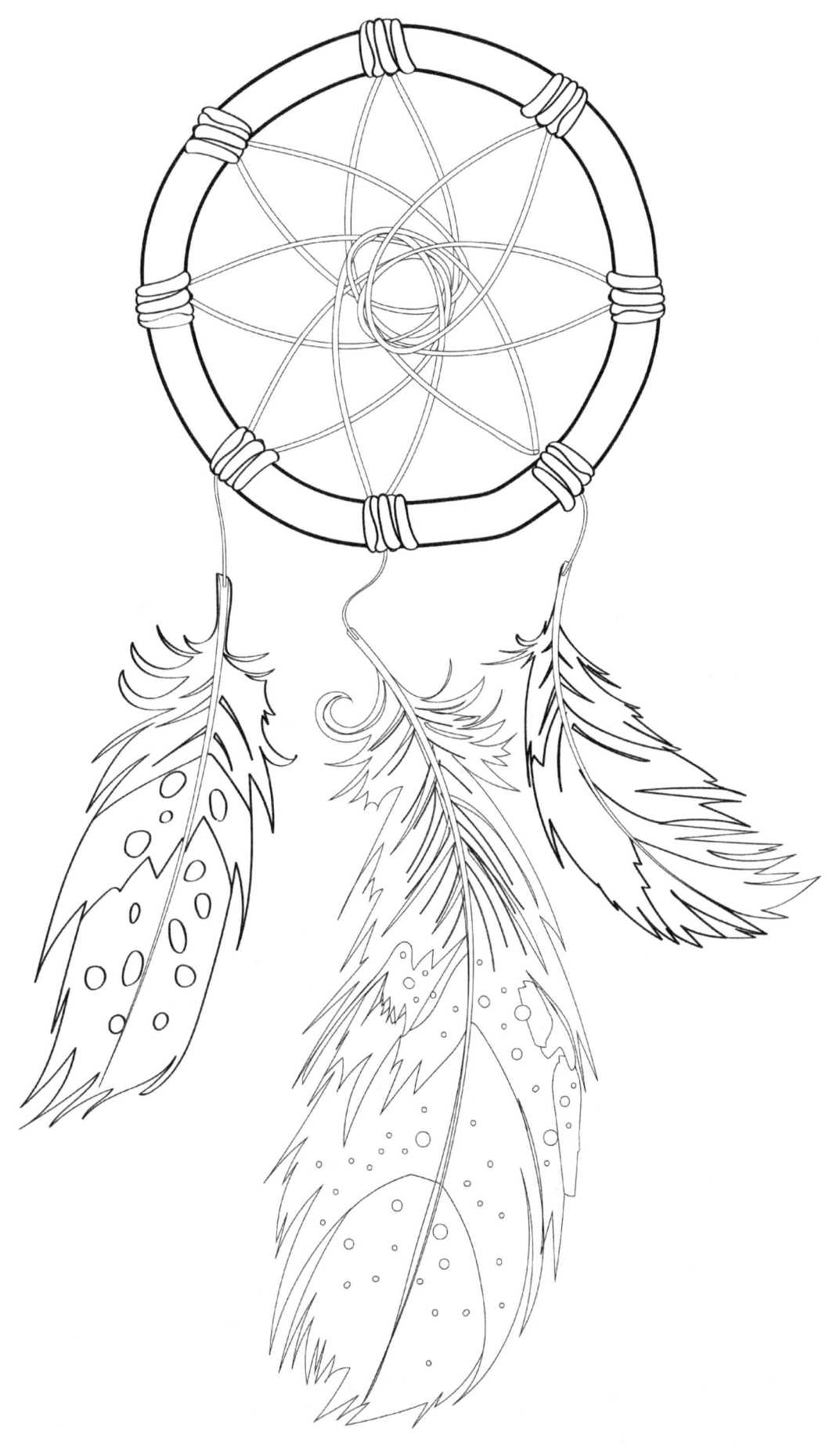

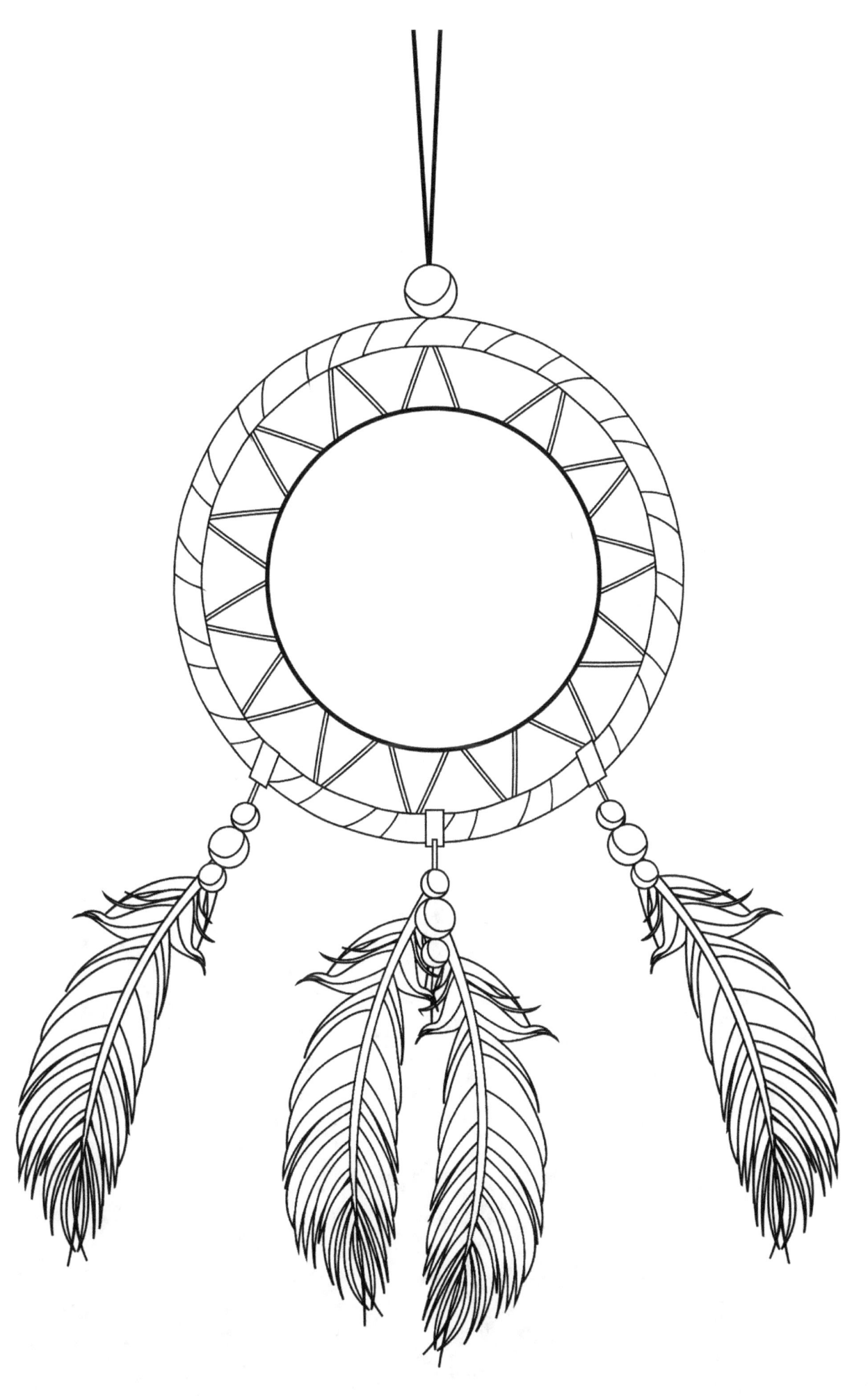

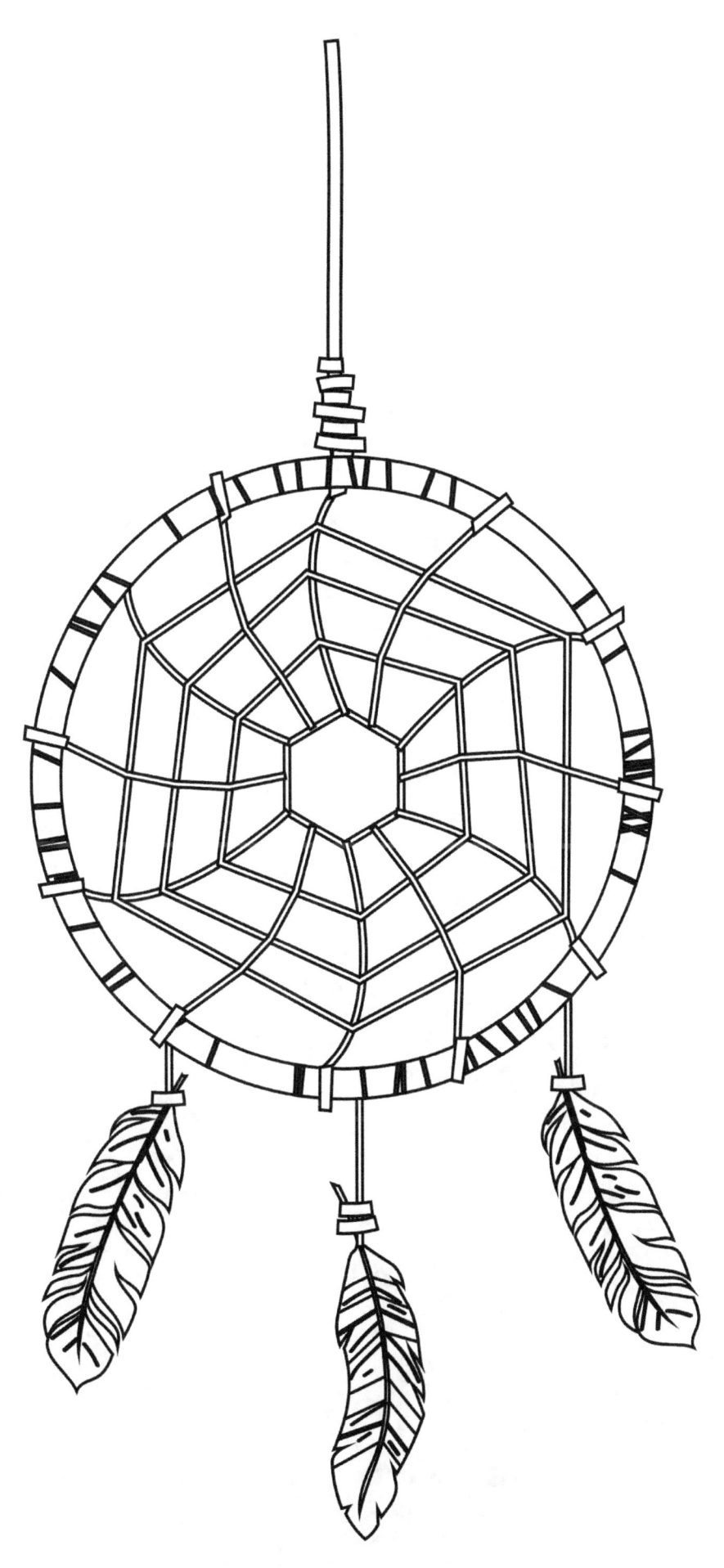

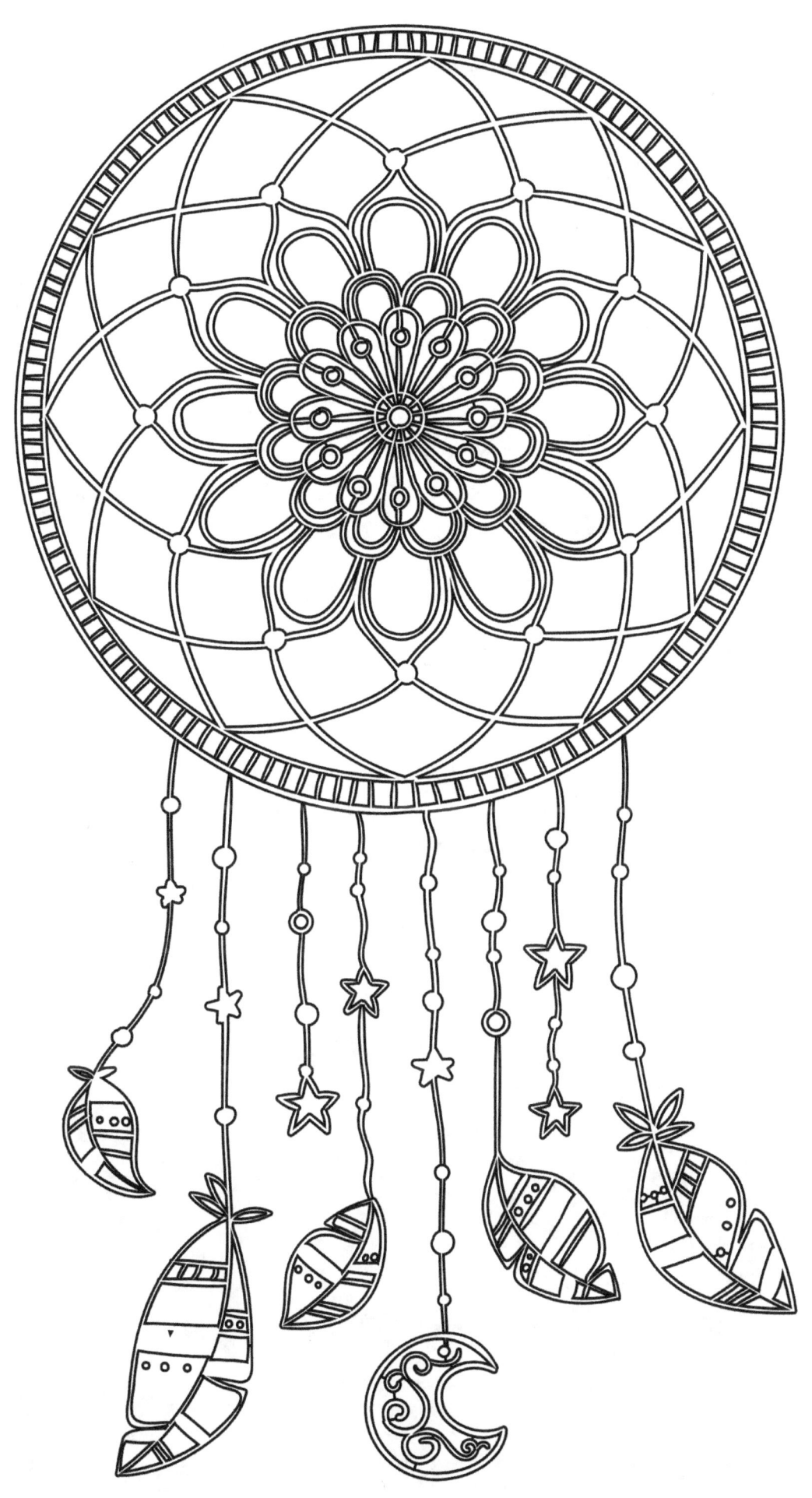

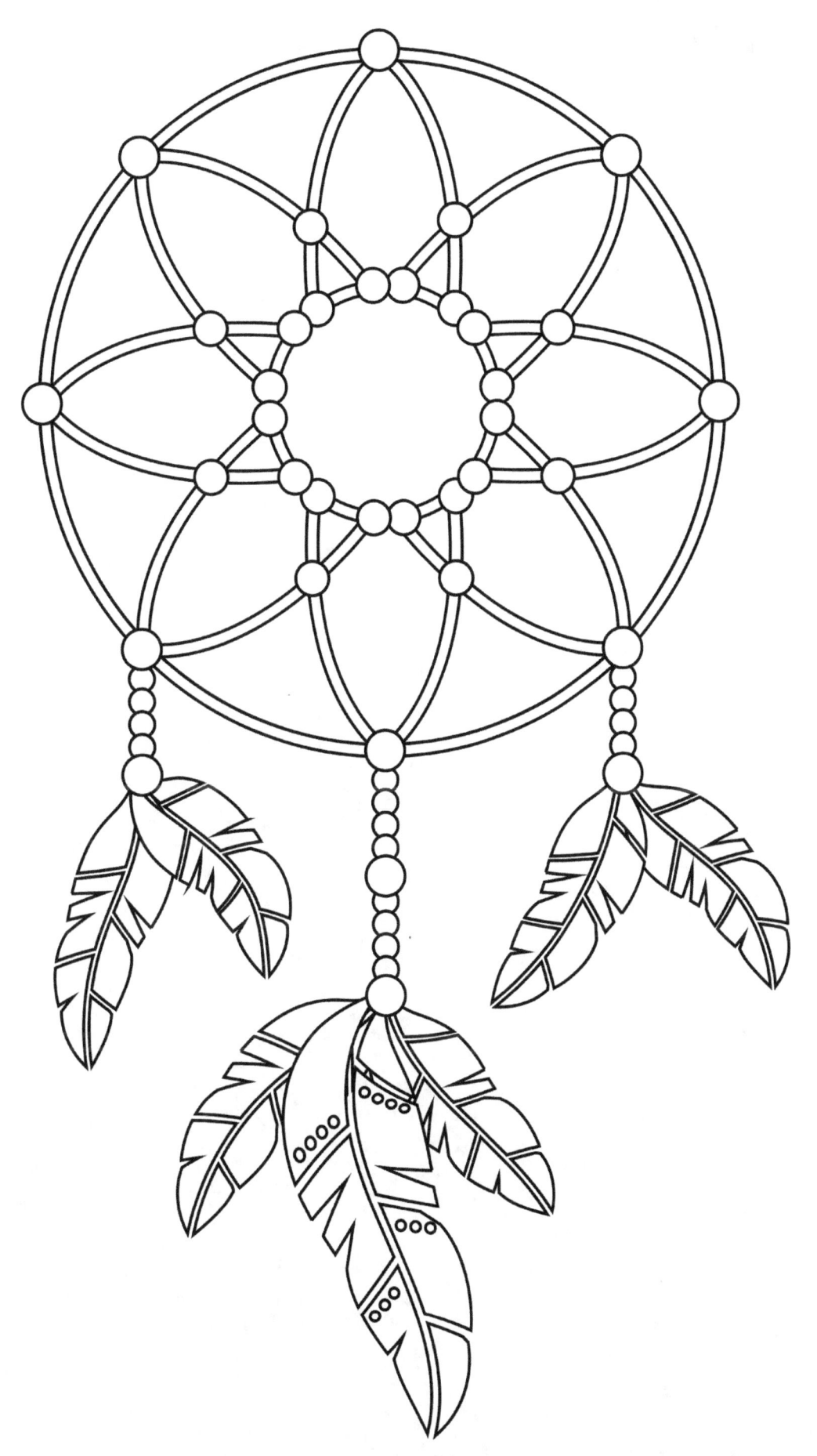

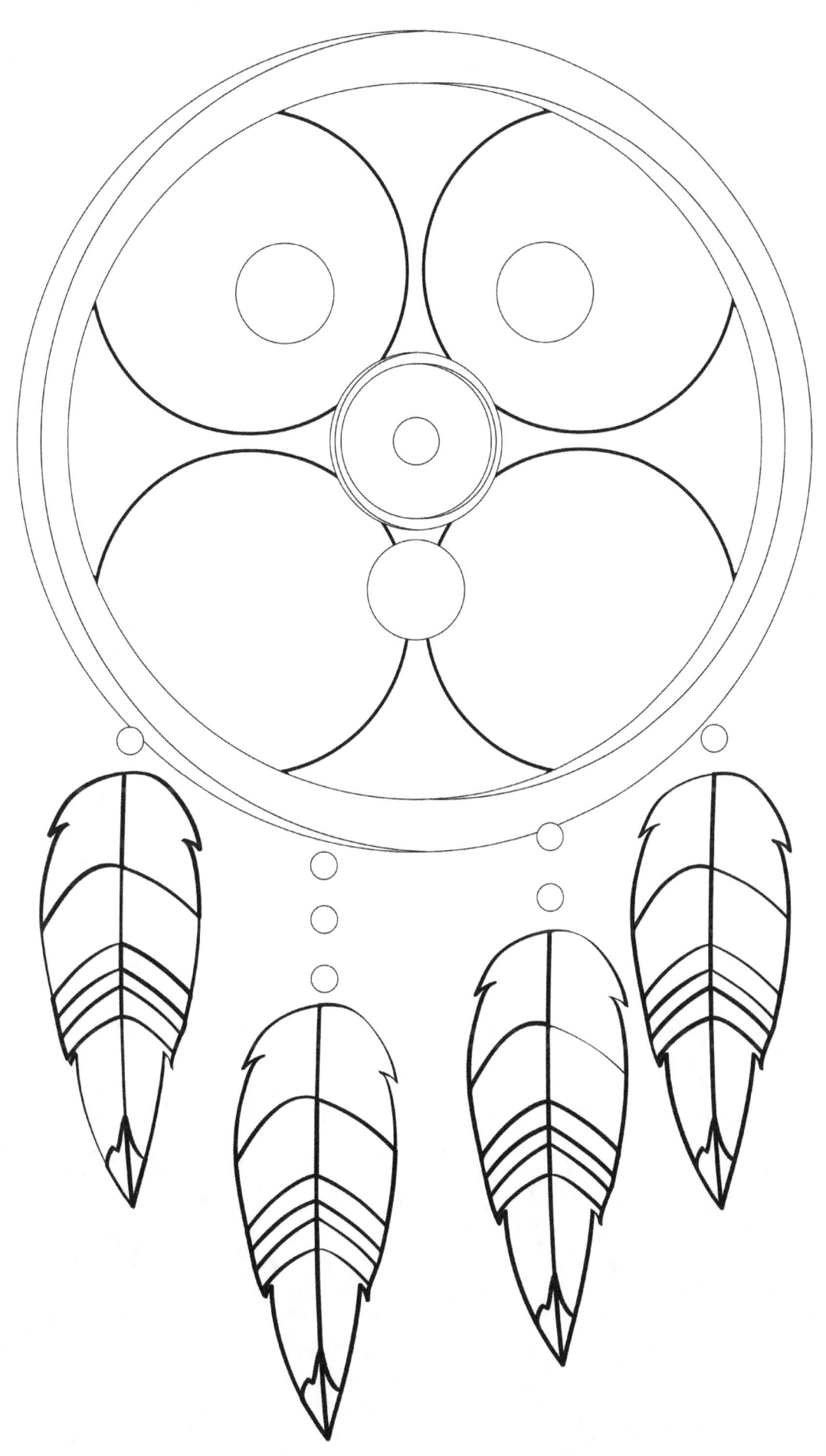

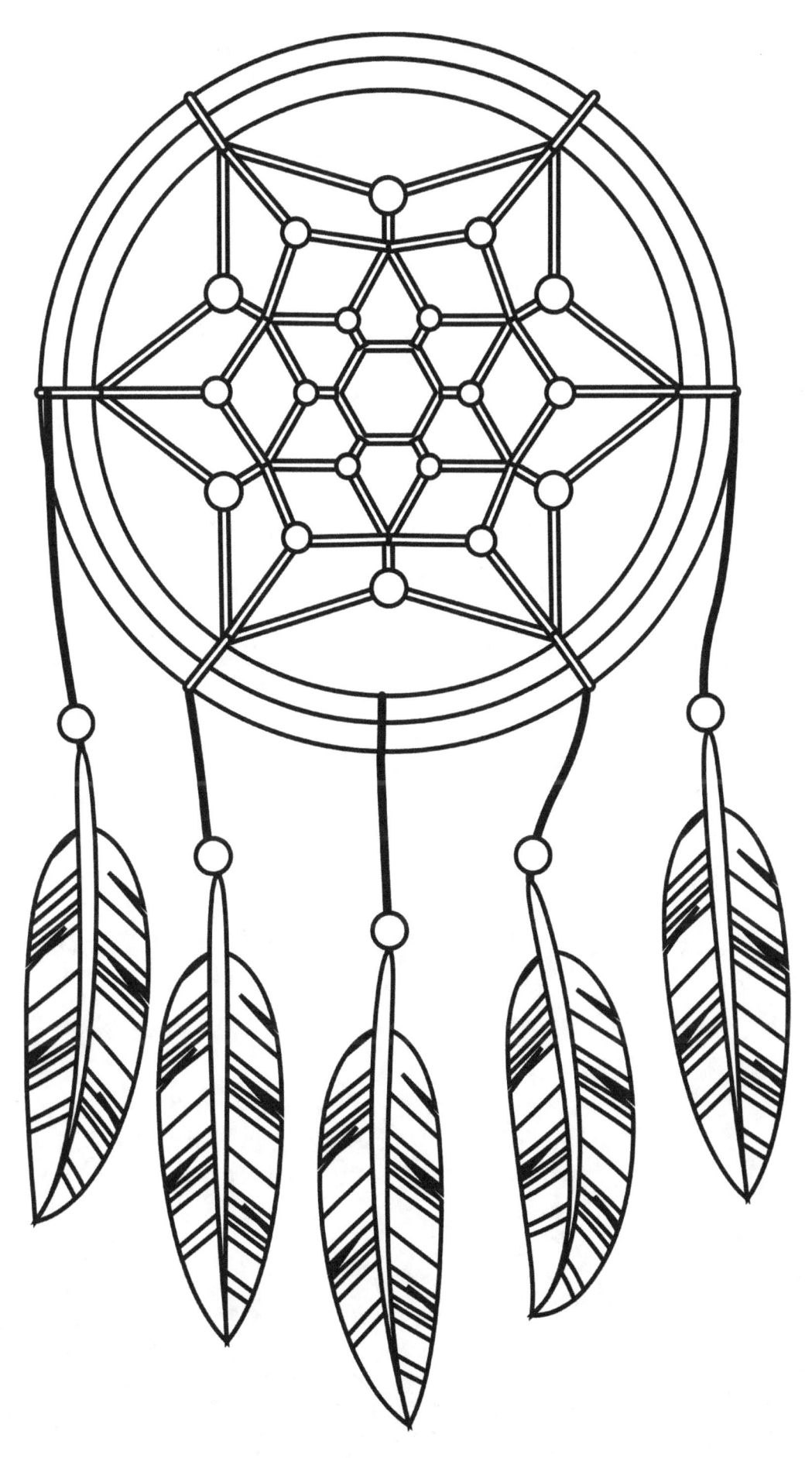

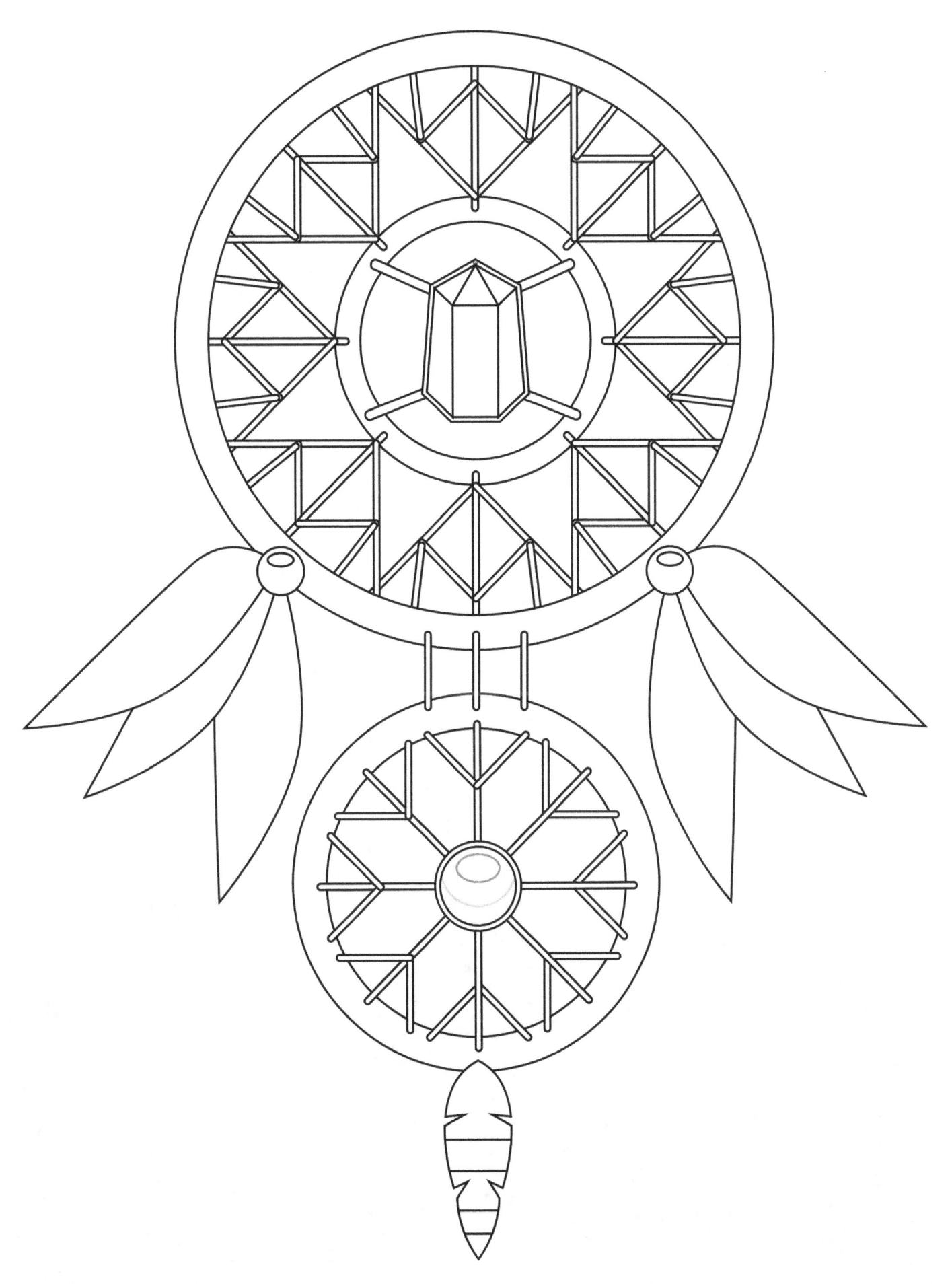

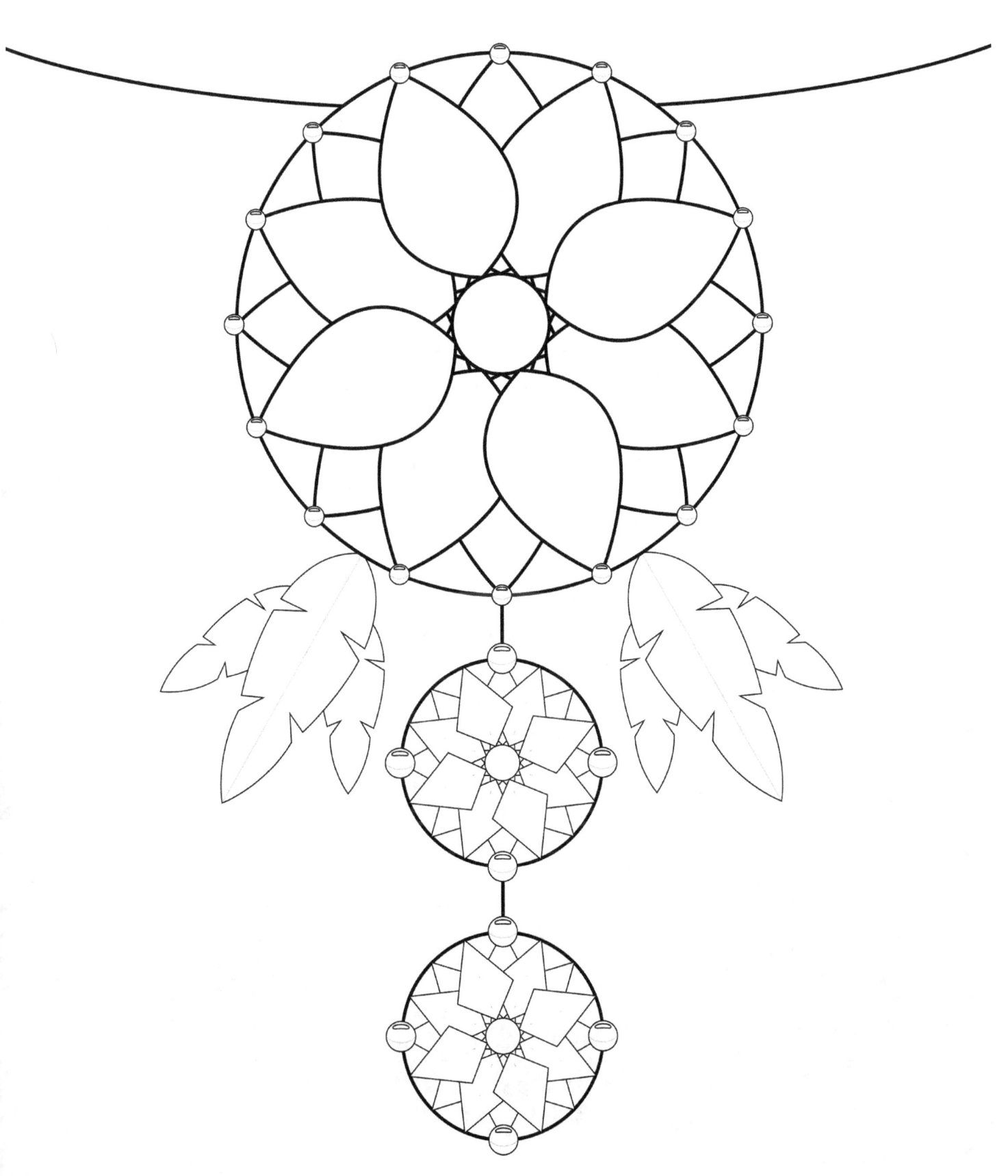

www.ingramcontent.com/pod-product-compliance
Lightning Source LLC
Chambersburg PA
CBHW080510220526
45465CB00006B/2440